Emotional

Blueprint

—A Book of Transformation—

How to Cultivate your Inner Voice

to help you Achieve Success

in all Aspects of Life

Lulu Baba

Printed in the USA

ISBN 978-1-5136-6151-3

www.LuluBabaBooks.com

Twitter: @LuluBabaBooks
Instagram: @LuluBabaBooks
Facebook.com/LuluBabaBooks

ACKNOWLEDGMENTS

Warmest regards to Dr. Ackerman and Dr. Kealy. You have helped me connect through multiple platforms with the source from which the mystery reveals itself.

Dr. Kirchner, you are a true friend.

A. Carpenter, thank you for all your help.

Special thanks to my wife, Brooke, who encouraged me to write this book while pushing me to describe the messages within in ways which would relate to as many people as possible.

Though we have never physically met, I acknowledge the Shaman who guides me through spirit quests.

I acknowledge the area which circumnavigates our planet, the space in and around our equator where Mother Nature blooms with ancient and new potential, primordial possibilities which echo the past and sing into the future.

I acknowledge the shadow and the light, the Earth and the Heavens, the death and the re-birth—of all things—and of course, the aspect within myself which mirrors it all.

CONTENTS

DISCLAIMER

This book is not medical advice. If you feel you have a medical condition which this book touches on, I strongly encourage you to seek professional medical advice and services. This book and its author are not responsible for the medical ideas you gather and substitute for state and federally approved medical advice and services. This book is not intended for the purpose of diagnosis or treatment of any illness or medical condition. Seek professional medical help if you believe you are suffering from a medical condition.

Purpose

The purpose of this book is to encourage and promote the building of healthy relationships and the bridging of gaps between people. Hopefully, the pages within this book will inspire and motivate you to ask the questions necessary to access, embrace, and develop your unique emotional blueprint. Through the development of your emotional blueprint you will be able to reveal the purpose you were born to share with the world. To stimulate your emotional growth, this book will push you to expand your boundaries.

The great intention of this book is to encourage you to try and build a relationship with that which seems to oppose you instead of trying to eradicate, defile or prove what is right and what is wrong. In this process, we may come to find that we have more in common (especially in areas of debate) with each other and the world around us than expected. We may also find that different perspectives can make us better, stronger and smarter.

This book is about emotional transformation; turning pain into joy, darkness into light, and fear into love. We needn't be stuck in fear, lost in doubt, or overwhelmed with anxiety. We can take the energy which seems to be holding us back and limiting our potential—the energy which can rob us of our health—and transform it into a new form of energy, a healing energy which can realign us with our purpose so we can continue to grow and evolve in the cycle of elevation.

We will be talking about the mystery in this book. The mystery refers to the mystery of life, the limitless potential and infinite possibilities of existence itself. A life filled with so much potential—infinite possibilities—can produce countless perspectives which can create cognitive dissonance. If you are having trouble with how a concept in this book is presented, then take the time to define your version of truth in relation to your version of reality. For example, if you don't agree with how love is expressed within this book, then seek to understand your own definition and perspective of love. In the process of finding your truth, just try and not crystallize your interpretation of love into some doctrine which will ultimately limit your experience of love. Instead, try to expand upon your perception of love.

From your unique version and definition of a concept, like love, explore all the possibilities of what love can be. Through emotional intelligence, you will be able to widen the boundaries of what love means to you as you mature alongside the healthy boundaries of your unique emotional blueprint. Healthy boundaries which are able to grow organically will broaden your definition of love.

Exploring the possibilities of what love can be will elevate your relationship with love, and in turn, will help to reveal the mystery of existence itself.

Everything in this book is a glimpse at the mystery. Although this book attempts to convey the mystery in some way, shape, or form what is important is for you to expand the mystery through your own unique perspective, as every perspective is valid.

Everyone is searching for something—on a journey which may seem to flow effortlessly one moment and then may seem blocked and painfully forsaken the next. Whether we are searching for a partner, a place, a child, a god, a new scientific discovery, a pet, or for something else, there is a common thread in our shared search. That common thread is our desire to cultivate relationships which produce authentic connections. While we search for these divine connections we also wish to uncover and unleash our creative expression. It is our boundless creativity which will ultimately lead us to discover and expand our current limitations. Achieving the impossible always compels us to repeat the process over, and over, and over again. Elevation is our nature. The emotional cycles we go through to mature and elevate is what we will explore.

All is Fair

Though this book is about emotions, it is in no way intended to promote weakness or advocate the notion that a person is in any way required to cater to the emotional demands of another.

One should not impose upon or inhibit the emotional freedom and creativity of others; however, there should never be any requirement or law which forces one to compromise his or her own beliefs or emotions for the emotional wellbeing of another.

It would be great if people considered the emotional health of others before they acted, but only if it were manifested through free will and choice, not governed by force of law.

Life is not fair. We learn through adversity and pain. We do not grow by refusing to acknowledge that which we do not understand.

This book is meant to promote emotional understanding, fortitude, endurance and resilience. It should never be used in any way to manipulate others to be more sensitive to your emotional needs.

Only do unto others what you would have done unto you.

For humankind to elevate as a species, we must learn to expand our emotions and not be so quick to blame external circumstances or others for what and how we are feeling.

Enslavement in any form can block the flow of emotions—emotions which are necessary to keep us expanding and in alignment with the cycle of elevation.

Accept responsibility and emotional accountability for what you are feeling. For whatever circumstance you find yourself in, in almost all cases, you carry the majority, if not all of the liability for whatever you are enduring.

The changing of eras brings about a changing of magic.

It is not an end, but a new cycle of elevation.

Introduction

This book is about our emotions and expanding the spectrum of existence. We will talk about love, energy, light, and joy, as well as magic, transformation, the shadow, black holes and alternate dimensions. We will also discuss God, nature, freedom, evolution, language, frequency, music, healing, and among other things; *the mystery* which unites everything within a dynamic existence.

Through this book you will hopefully learn how to cultivate your inner voice and transform your life to live with meaning and purpose. You will learn about the stages in the cycle of elevation and the complementary forces which guide us to discover our unique emotional blueprint.

This book is designed for you to question. The concepts held within the pages of this book are just that, concepts, no crystallized doctrines or absolute answers live within this book. Instead, this book encourages you to cultivate your genius creativity—it begs you to ask questions—questions which will help develop and broaden your unique perspective of *the mystery* of life. Although this book tries to convey some form, some understanding of *the mystery* within a structured system, what's more important is for you to expand *your* understanding of *the mystery* through your own unique perspective, therefore, not everything about *the mystery* conveyed in this book will be answered in the details you may desire. It's everyone's responsibility to build upon *the mystery* by adding their own unique perspective; that is the way *the mystery* works.

Every perspective is valid.

Don't try too hard to create a concrete version of *the mystery* for it is ever evolving and elevating. The magic and the allure of *the mystery* dwells within its elusiveness.

Many of the concepts discussed in this book are linked to other concepts which are discussed in later chapters. Not everything is explained all at once; concepts which are presented in earlier chapters may be touched on again and explained in greater detail in later chapters. If they are not, then it is up to you to ask the necessary questions which will allow you to build upon the concepts yourself. It is your responsibility to reveal and grow *the mystery* in new ways. Expand the perspective of the collective human consciousness as it is authentically revealed to you through your own unique emotional blueprint.

Again, every perspective is valid. Every perspective builds upon *the mystery*; that is the way *the mystery* works.

At times this book will seem to be repetitive. Repetition is a natural method which helps us to learn and grow with ease. The sun rises and sets, the moon rises and sets, the seasons change and repeat. Every cycle is a reflection of the grand cycle of elevation. What is revealed within this book will be repeated again and again in as many new, different, and creative ways as possible to learn and re-learn concepts in much the same way we experience and re-experience the cycle of life in new and different ways.

The cycle of life, the circle of life, the cycle of elevation, *the mystery*, infinity, God, etc., are all words, disciplines, and concepts which share a similar goal—a common thread—of expanding the connection and experience of existence itself.

If you are having any difficulty with any of the concepts presented within this book, then perhaps it is something you won't be able to come to understand logically. You may have to wait for life to allow you to relate to these concepts through your own experience.

Once you build a connection through experience and create an emotional bridge to what you seek to understand, then you will awaken the force, the gravity which has always bonded you to it: love.

The concepts within this book are but a basis for you to grow—a platform for you to expand upon so you may discover who you are and reveal your emotional blueprint more and more, for your emotional blueprint is like *the mystery* itself: elusive and infinite.

Portraits of Time

A picture shows you what was; a mirror shows you what is; a dream reveals what could be; while relationships expand all possibilities.

Do not read the pages of this book the same way you would look at a picture.

Do not mimic the messages within like you would gaze into a mirror.

Do not get lost in the fantasy of a dream that could be.

Apply the concepts you find useful in this book to discover your potential, your inner voice.

Connect to the source of your energy—the motivation behind your inner voice—so you may discover your unique emotional blueprint. The source of your energy will reveal the purpose you were born to share with the world. Your purpose is the gift that will broaden the experience of this gift we call life.

A picture, a mirror, and a dream are all images, perceptions and projections of the past, the present, and the future. The limitation these three aspects of time share is a visage of inaction. Action is what is required, what is necessary to transform vision into reality.

Don't sit around and contemplate the words of this book or the philosophy of its teachings.

Act.

Experience what could be by manifesting your dreams into reality. True vision creates and produces purpose. Purpose is revealed by no other means than action.

What you do, what you set into motion through decisive action, is what reflects purpose in your life. Life can add up to cheap thrills or valuable experiences. Our actions will dictate a life of substance or of insignificance.

We create our pictures, we look into the mirror every day, and we dream for something which will resonate with us as meaning, yet we will never experience this connection or cultivate a relationship with our purpose if we do not act.

We mustn't hide in the safety and security of neutrality or mediocrity; we must risk it all in the face of adversity and rejection with the will to overcome any and all obstacles so our purpose and greatness may be revealed.

It's only when we merge with our meaning that we are able to accept the past, understand the present and integrate the future to form an elevated vision of purpose, which compels us into action toward a perpetual dream. A transcendent voyage: The cycle of elevation.

A Joyful Meaning

Though will is necessary, meaning shall not be achieved through force of will alone.

Though flow is necessary, meaning cannot come about through

just ease of flow.

Rivers may gently carve out the easiest path to the ocean, but the mountains which feed the rivers were formed through the force of friction and the will of action. It is the complementary forces of nature working together which decorate our world in such lush and vibrant hues. It is this beauty sculpted through the playful interaction between friction and flow which eventually revealed our planet's meaning and purpose: relationships which support life.

Meaning is discovered and harnessed through a paradox of chaotic discipline, an effort which is both playful and challenging. Meaning is a symphony orchestrated and composed by a labor of love. This gravity of love shall effortlessly bring together the components necessary to build a relationship and forge a connection; a connection which completes a circuit and sets into motion the motivational energy (the will and action) required to unite all that could be, so that we may harvest that which lights up the soul: joy.

The Cycle of Elevation

The cycle of elevation is a form of cognitive behavioral therapy (CBT) in that the cycle of elevation is a concept which seeks to transform how we perceive the world and our difficulties through our emotions. The cycle of elevation asks for us to first accept the current patterns in our life—patterns which influence our emotions and affect the perception of our potential.

The second stage in the cycle of elevation seeks to understand the patterns which influence us. These patterns are studied in relation to our feelings and thoughts, for it is through our feelings and thoughts (perception) that we are able to transform what we believe to be our potential into our reality. The structure of our beliefs (belief structure) form how we expect the world to operate and exist. We must come to understand not just our own belief structure, but the belief structure of others so we may interact with one other with a certain degree of diplomacy.

The third stage tends to be the hardest as the cycle of elevation asks for us to integrate the perspectives we have developed of the world—our formed beliefs and expectations—with the perspectives, beliefs, and expectations of others. Only by integrating the perspectives, beliefs, and expectations of others, are we able to form the relationships necessary to unite and align our emotions with all life and the grand cycle of existence itself. The ability to build bridges into other worlds, other beliefs, and align with the expectations of all life, allows us to tap into the energy and emotion of the grand spectrum of existence: joy.

From joy we can elevate and come to rest with new enchantments. These spells are woven into the very fabric—magic—of life and existence itself. In this stage, we evolve and expand our potential to begin the cycle anew with an elevated perspective.

Accept, understand, integrate, and elevate.

Broadening Definitions and Expanding Labels

The cycle of elevation is similar to cognitive behavioral therapy in another way. Each stage in the cycle of elevation is essentially a short-term goal which requires problem-solving in a hands-on way to reach the next stage in the cycle; a cycle which is self-perpetuating and ever moving toward a transcendent purpose.

Labels help us define our world. The goal of our emotional blueprint and the cycle of elevation is to help re-define ourselves and the world through broadening our definitions and expanding the labels in which we perceive life itself.

Though the cycle of elevation holds many parallels to cognitive behavioral therapy, the cycle of elevation is ultimately its own concept, thus, I will not be referencing the similarities between the cycle of elevation and CBT within this book often, or possibly not at all, for the similarities are implied. Just as this book is a form of energy medicine and emotional transformation, I will not be referencing the aspects of this book which are related to energy medicine or emotional transformation often, or possibly not at all, for the similarities are again, implied.

Stage 1: Spring-Potential-Dawn-Acceptance

Stage one is where we will begin. Here, we will lay the foundation of the emotional blueprint and the inner voice. If there is a beginning, potential seems like a great place to start. Stage one will teach the basic principles of the cycle of elevation. The cycle of elevation is what helps our emotional blueprint grow, mature, and blossom. The cycle of elevation is a process much like that of the seasons.

Spring brings potential for new life, new growth, and new possibilities. Stage one is the dawn of a new day. We begin the cycle of elevation with acceptance, the acceptance of what-is in relation to the potential of who we are.

Chapter 1

Emotional Relevance

Chapter one is all about the relevance of emotion in our lives. Emotions help shape our perspective of the world. In life, no matter how logical we become, we only ever experience life through emotion.

The Relevance of Emotional Intelligence

Why is emotional intelligence relevant?

Emotional intelligence is relevant because our emotions are in direct correlation with how we view and interact with the world.

My perception of the truth and your perception of the truth may share some similarities, but the nuances which make my perspective unique from yours, and your perspective unique from mine originate from the varying levels of emotion that we attach to different aspects of a shared reality.

A great example would be if you were lost in the forest with a stranger. While you may be frightened and anxious about the situation, the other person might be excited and eager for the adventure of surviving in the wild (or vice-versa).

Another example of unique perspectives on display would be after a crime (or any event involving a group of spectators for that matter). When witnesses are cross-examined using standardized questions about the way events unfolded, assuming all witnesses were fully present during the occurrence, and all witnesses upheld the highest code of honesty and integrity, each witness would still have a slightly different story or version of how the situation developed, matured, and concluded.

Each of us experiences reality in a slightly different way. The key word is experience.

Our emotions help govern and influence our thoughts. In turn, our thoughts manifest a unique and distinct perception of reality, which we encounter as an alternate experience when compared to the shared reality of a circumstance or situation.

In my experience, most people think of reality as a constant—a shared experience of existence which doesn't and shouldn't change from person to person.

To feel secure, I believe humans have a need to create some sort of construct which is both specific and finite out of the shared reality we all experience. The platform we create serves as an unwavering measure of truth. From this structure we build our individual realities.

In a twilight-zone sort of way, each person lives and operates in his or her own personal dimension. Your version of reality may have some similarities to mine, but the subtle differences in the way you attach your emotions to certain scenarios, and the subtle differences in the way I attach my emotions to certain scenarios will ultimately influence, affect, and alter the way you and I respond to each other in our so-called "shared" reality. This makes your version of our "shared" reality slightly and sometimes dramatically different from mine.

When I meet a stranger, if the conversation goes further than pleasantries and superficial small talk, then the next step in our relationship involves testing out how we feel in each other's world. We dance with words and toss ideas back and forth like playing catch. What we are essentially doing is comparing and contrasting one another's perception of reality. If our emotions respond in a similar fashion to the theoretical scenarios we produce in conversation, then our realities will tend to mesh well together. If we are able to establish a connection, if we are able to find an emotional counterpart in one another, then we will be able to move forward in the relationship building process.

If our emotions don't line up while conjuring up some pretend reality, then our perception of one another could simply be that we are different. If there are too many differences in our individual realities then we tend not to move forward in the relationship building process. We avoid making a connection because our worlds seem too different to form a relationship. A relationship is what is necessary to bridge our worlds together so we can establish a connection with one another.

When our realities seem to oppose each other with a certain level of intensity, we tend to remain in our individual realities. We choose to move forward separately, without a connection or emotional bridge which would help to integrate the worlds we live in.

Without the connection, the emotional bridge to unite our realities, our emotions can start to overwhelm us, especially if we are forced to work with each other in any way. When your reality cracks the foundation of my reality, and my reality shakes the constructs of your reality, we both look to defend our realms as our worlds collide. As we both prepare for war, our walls and shields are brought up, and so too are our weapons. We begin to fight each other in the hope of destroying the views, beliefs, and principals which threaten the foundation on which we base our lives.

The sad part is that while we seek to destroy what we believe to be "bad", or "untrue" in regard to our own perspectives, what we are actually doing is trying to rid each other of the uniqueness which makes an individual who they are.

The vibrant aspect responsible for the beauty of every human being is the unique perspective of reality which stems from his or her exceptional, one-of-a-kind, emotional blueprint. Our emotional blueprint is also the seat of our creativity, a unique expression of self which human beings were born to share. You can almost say that a person's purpose is birthed from his or her emotional blueprint. Our emotional blueprint is our gift, our offering to the world.

As exciting as all of this may sound, this is where healthy boundaries come in to play.

The Establishment of Healthy Boundaries

Why do we need Healthy Boundaries?

You have a right to live just as I have a right to live.

Your emotions matter, just as mine do. Your views, opinions, and beliefs matter just as mine do.

I have a right to live and operate within the constructs of my so-called perspective or "dimension of reality" just as you do, but neither of us has the right to force anyone to conform to a certain way of being or living, just as we should never be forced to surrender our own way of being or living. I shall not force my ways, beliefs, traditions or religions on you, just as you shall not force your ways, beliefs, traditions or religions on me.

The next part may be hard to swallow, but just because you live a certain way doesn't mean I have to agree or support your way of living.

I don't owe you anything.

No one owes you anything.

The world owes you nothing.

No one owes anyone anything except respect.

Here is why.

I reject the idea that reality is a constant. This will be expanded upon more in later chapters with quantum mechanics. This is where you and I may agree in some aspects and disagree in others. If this is the case, instead of seeing my perspective as an attack on yours, and your perspective as an attack on mine, we may try instead to see the beauty in both perspectives.

There are so many different ways of being, so many different perspectives of reality which bring beauty into the world in slightly different ways. We should ask ourselves why any "one" way or perspective should be adopted as the pinnacle of truth and existence, especially if the "one" way or perspective is our own.

If you and I can view the different beliefs of humankind as beautiful, in a similar way we might see a tiger as beautiful, with respect to the animal's power, grace and deadliness, then we bestow upon each other the greatest honor of all: respect.

Neither you nor I may never want to interact with a tiger, but when we grant respect to the tiger and her place in the world, we give her meaning. Respect allows an individual to uncover and execute his or her meaning in life, to find and live his or her own purpose.

Asking a tiger to live the way we think she should live won't end well for either of us. Imposing a way of life which is outside the parameters of her design will not only destroy the tiger, but it will also shatter any possibility of establishing a harmonious relationship with her.

This is where you and I differ from a tiger. Nature exists in reality, but nature is far from an unwavering constant.

Nature is a cycle of growth and change which embodies a mystery, a mystery of both the possibility of something and the possibility of nothing simultaneously. The platform of existence, of life itself, is constantly moving, shifting, growing, evolving and elevating in a grand cycle.

Unlike a tiger who can only exist and interact in the world within the parameters of her design, humans have evolved and elevated further than the constructs of general reality. We are not confined to the code of nature the way plants and animals are.

A tiger is a link in a chain which helps make up the web of life.

Though we do not know for sure, but it seems a tiger is completely fulfilled in only operating to the extent of her design.

The tiger does not seem to dream of venturing beyond her parameters of existence, and thus, does not comprehend she is only but a link in the web of life, a tiny piece in a seemingly infinite puzzle. She does not seem to consciously understand her influence in the ultimate experience of existence.

Humans, on the other hand, do.

Humans have discovered and categorized many links and threads in the web of life. We wish to organize everything as if life were just strands of data, labeling anything and everything which may help to reinforce the logical platform on which we base existence (the funny part is that existence is not just data-based, but a combination of both data and experience-based relationships).

We seek to discover and push the boundaries of meaning, purpose and limits. We do this with everything we encounter, and extend it even further through our imagination, desires and dreams.

We want to know the "why" of everything, including ourselves.

This is how and why I have come to believe that there is a force greater than myself, and yes, I am talking about God, but not in the way you might think.

God

For me, God, in terms of religion, is just another manufactured belief structure which we project onto our individual versions of reality.

There are many old and established religions which claim the throne of righteousness, purity, and ultimate salvation in human existence. While these religions have many valuable virtues and ethical lessons to share with the world, I still view them as I do a tiger: with respect.

Organized religion has a place in the world and there is much meaning brought to light because of their existence, but I treat organized religion as a powerful, graceful, and deadly tiger who can cut through my existence with one swipe of her paw.

For me, human potential lies in the mystery.

As stated earlier, I believe humans have evolved and elevated a bit beyond the confines of general reality. I know this because I understand why and how my individual link can influence not just the web of life, but the web of existence itself (it all has to do with cycles).

I am able to call forth an idea of how I want to live, and with enough creativity, resources and motivation, manifest that idea into reality.

You and I have the ability to create our own version of reality. From the perspective of all other creatures on our planet, we have super powers. The problem with all this power is that the majority of people in the world still don't quite yet know how to fully harness this ability or understand what to focus their divine gift on.

So much power and the freedom to use or squander it all on

whatever we desire can make us feel lost, empty, and sometimes, alone. If we don't have a guide or blueprint to help us understand our why, our purpose, and our potential, we can tend to feel pretty helpless and hopeless at times.

Our why, our purpose, and the understanding of our potential is what we seek so earnestly in life; the Holy Grail, so to speak.

This book will slowly reveal how we can discover a path which will help us understand our why, our purpose, and our potential, so that we can create and establish a connection with all life, with existence itself.

Even without the knowledge of our why, purpose, or potential, even in a state of ignorance, our parameters and potential far exceed that of a tiger, and I believe, much further than any "one" organized religion can take us.

Still, I believe in a force greater than myself because I observe nature. As soon as you think you understand how nature works, as soon as you believe you have uncovered the laws of nature, she surprises you and breaks through the structure you have confined her in.

Human beings are just one example of nature surprising existence with a creation which defies any of the rules or laws we bestow upon her. We ourselves don't even fit the steady design of nature that we project onto her.

This is how I view God, the force greater than myself—a mystery which defies structure but also creates structure at the same time. God, to me, is the possibility of something and the possibility of nothing all at once. Just like nature.

It is the sum of all the alternate realities created and projected by mankind which saturate the world with such beautiful and vibrant hues. It is because I believe differences create a more beautiful world that I am inclined to respect another person's version of reality. If we reject all versions of reality other than our own, then we are unable to grow and elevate ourselves. We will be unable to see and experience the full spectrum of life and existence.

Still, healthy boundaries are important because if we give up our own reality for another's acceptance or love, or for the promise of salvation, we deny the force within ourselves which mirrors God. When we give up our own version of reality, we choke and ultimately restrain our own infinite potential and creativity. Our unique hue is denied a place to shine in the spectrum of life, narrowing the way existence can be experienced.

Repressing our creativity silences our unique emotional blueprint, our gift to the world, which if cultivated correctly and respected properly, leads to the ability to construct not just a distinct and beautiful version of reality, but authentic connections which can bridge even the most difficult emotional perspectives together through respectful and loving relationships. These respectful and loving relationships can eventually unite all realities, elevating not only ourselves, but humankind and consciousness as a whole.

Elevating our consciousness brings us closer to God, so we may better understand our purpose. Purpose reveals what to focus our divine ability and power on so we can feel not just fulfilled, but connected.

The Spectrum of Love and God

Love isn't a one-dimensional concept; neither is God.

No discipline or religion can define or contain either concept within the confines of a label or structure, nor define the parameters of infinite potential in which love and God operate.

This may be to the disbelief of many, but in my perspective, God, like love, is repelled by worship and doesn't take kindly to being chased. When you place others you desire on a pedestal and hold them as some sacred being, they tend to view you as a being of lesser value and unworthy of their affection.

People we seek to love who are perceived as perfect and the reason for our beating heart—tend to run in the opposite direction of our advances very quickly, and with good reason.

God, like love, desires respect, not worship.

Love, like God, desires not perfection, but acceptance.

When we align our intentions and seek to accept, understand and integrate love, we elevate our consciousness in a way which mirrors or reflects divinity. This is because we are choosing to build a relationship with what-is, with the reality-of, instead of a concept, belief, or projection of what we desire. When we accept unconditionally, the "mystery," the grand spectrum of love itself opens up to us.

The "mystery" is a concept which ignites our emotions to pursue and develop the potential of our consciousness.

Our individual consciousness, cultivated properly, manifests our unique version of reality into the world, which, when united with the consciousness of others, spans and encompasses the collective potential of joy and love, the forces behind energy and gravity—the flow and friction, the yin and yang, the complementary frequencies responsible for breathing life into the entire multi-verse.

God and love don't take kindly to the act of being put on a pedestal and worshiped, for the simple reason that doing so places them so far out of reach that it makes it impossible to unite with them.

If the embodiment of love and God is truly our purpose—if love and God reflect our passion and desire for connection—then the source of that power and mystery would be far closer than the unobtainable position we place them in.

Love and God are far more attainable than we think because the ability to build a relationship requires—or necessitates—the ability to relate. We cannot relate to something which we are chasing. If we pursue something with the belief that we will never be able to reach it, then we have already lost it. If we are unable to comprehend the source of which we wish to connect with, then it will take on the cloak of legend, and may as well become as phony as a fairytale. A belief structure based on the concept that a relationship with love and God will always remain out of our grasp, can generate the type of emotions and behaviors which keep us feeling unworthy, alone, and empty.

We need to believe we are worthy, connected and full of both love and God so we can manifest respectful relationships with the divine aspects of all things. The ability to relate in one way or another, to the divine virtues of love and god within everything, will extinguish the illusion which keeps us apart. The illusion of separateness. Once the myth of separateness is lifted, we are then free to establish authentic relationships with one another and build the emotional bridges necessary to connect to a higher understanding, an elevated consciousness which will reveal and expand the mystery of love and God within us all.

When we seek to pair with a partner in the name of love, whether it be of the opposite or the same sex, we seek to accept, understand, and integrate an aspect of love, of God, which we don't quite yet understand and are unable to connect with through our own means.

What we truly desire in a relationship with another is the unification of complements to produce a force, an energy that would unite the alternate realities we seek to understand in one another so we may truly come together. Through the merger of alternate realities we hope to compose a broader definition of love while elevating ourselves and each other to achieve a new potential of consciousness.

Together, we wish to become more than we could ever hope to be alone. We come together to give birth to better versions of ourselves and give rise to the possibility of a deeper understanding of love and God. A deeper understanding of anything, especially love and God, expands our consciousness, and when we elevate consciousness, we elevate existence itself.

The Spectrum of Existence

One of the most marvelous phenomena of existence, is the vast spectrum in which life is revealed.

You could take all that I have written thus far and argue that my points are invalid and have no merit, no substance or claim in truth.

You can contend all my perspectives with debate. You can argue that organized religion is the only structure keeping human beings civilized. You can make a case that organized religion in all its forms is responsible for the advancement of societies.

You can say that the virtues contained within organized religions are absolutely vital and necessary for establishing a hierarchy between peoples and nations, based on the morals and ethics of the religion they follow.

You can make a case that there is a God in the classical sense, and that God falls within the design of religion. Perhaps you have a way to prove that God is the master creator of the universe, whose sole purpose is to cherish humans above all other creatures until some prophesized judgement day, when the pure and righteous peoples of Earth will journey to live with this ultimate, divine creator for all eternity.

This is one valid version of reality, but there are so many more.

One could also conclude that religion and spirituality are all a collection of fantastic stories, fairy tales that lead people to forget who they are.

You could say that people who follow a religious or spiritual path give in to faith, and thus, give up all sense of logic, accountability, and facts.

You could make just as strong a case that science is the only real truth. You could say that reality is experienced in the moment and that each moment we are presented with requires active and decisive choices based on the data provided to improve upon the process of life.

Again, another valid version of reality.

In even another version of reality, someone may claim that existence is the byproduct of random events. Perhaps existence happened by chance and that the chaos of this existence was somehow organized to produce varying aspects of life in a hit-or-miss sort of way. Maybe there is no method to the madness of existence and life is some accidental and unplanned mess.

My point is that there are many varying degrees of realities, and they are all valid. Every reality, every theory can be proven true or useful at some time and in some way, but no reality or theory can be proven true all the time and in every way.

Every individual experiences the world, experiences existence in slightly different ways. These diverse and extraordinary experiences are due to our unique and individual emotional blueprints. We all have a truth to reveal and a creativity to share with the world that will beautify life and expand existence, but only if we respect the truth and creativity of all existence.

The Subconscious Gut

I would wager a large sum of money that as you read my version of reality and the theoretical realities I used as examples for the purpose of contrast, that you felt an emotional pull toward one reality and an emotional aversion to another.

Our gut knows where we thrive in the spectrum of existence. When we resonate with something or someone, we are able to form a bond, a deep connection with something or someone through the comprehension of another reality which parallels our own.

Comprehension is an acknowledgement of existence. There has to be some structure in order to organize the chaos (emotion/potential in the gut) in some way so that it is brought into comprehension, thus existing as a perspective. The brain is what processes and brings structure to emotion. The brain pulls the subconscious of emotion into consciousness. When the gut and the mind come together they form a perspective of consciousness or existence.

It is easier to comprehend that which reflects something within our emotional blueprint, something close to our emotional perception of reality. For example, if I enjoy eating healthy, staying fit, and the color purple, and a girl with purple hair walks into the gym eating a salad, I would be immediately attracted to her.

We are drawn to the tunes and melodies which mirror aspects of our own emotional blueprint. Our emotional blueprint is but one version of reality in the spectrum of existence. The spectrum of existence is composed of all versions of reality, the composition of all emotional blueprints, and not just humans. The collective consciousness of the universe is why existence is filled with endless potential and infinite possibilities.

In a sense, our emotional blueprint is born from a version or aspect of the spectrum of existence. From our gut we cultivate our emotional blueprint. If we are able to nurture our emotional blueprint through the cycle of elevation and allow it to evolve—to bloom and grow—we ignite new possibilities, weaving our unique potential into the web of life. Our expanded version of reality adds strands to the web and broadens the spectrum of existence itself.

I say gut because that is where our emotions dwell. Our gut is where the aspect (need and desire) which influences our emotional blueprint spring from.

The phrase "gut instinct" stems from our ancient, ancestral lineage that still persuades our higher consciousness to remain within the radius of its original design.

I am talking about instincts.

In fact, it is my belief that our subconscious dwells not in the mind, but in the gut. Again, this is not something that is proven, this is not scripture, do not take this book to be some religious relic or bible of some sort, this is just the way I view the world. What I hope and encourage you to do is to ethically build upon your own beliefs and perspectives, in a way which will always respect the lives of others. Ultimately your life is yours to do what you wish.

The reason I believe the gut is where the subconscious lives is because when the gut is compromised (hungry, infected, damaged … etc.) the mind is noticeably affected.

As a nurse, I have first-hand experience working with people who have had ailments that stemmed from the gut (excess acid, ulcers, tumors, blockages, infections… etc.), and the majority of these people also had noticeable changes in their mood. The ability to focus, concentrate and cope seemed to be affected to a much larger degree than a person suffering from an injury or illness not directly stemming from the gut. For example, a person with a broken arm or leg seemed way more cognizant than a person suffering from a pain in their gut due to a small bowel obstruction.

Aside from my own experiences, there are scientific, peer-reviewed studies showing the correlation between the health of the gut and the health of the mind.

There is a great book by Natasha Campbell-McBride, MD, called Gut and Psychology Syndrome that is backed by her experience, clinical studies, and research on the nutritional connections with psychiatric and neurological disorders.

If we think of the body as a vehicle, like a car, there is a lot of clinical-based evidence to support the idea that the gut may not only represent the engine, but is also the driver behind the wheel. While the mind, with all its complex and beautiful functions, is merely a fancy steering wheel.

My favorite reason I believe the gut is actually our subconscious in disguise is that when I eat something my stomach doesn't agree with, I have the most intense and weird dreams at night (humor).

Why this is all relevant and important is because the majority of our time is spent trying to balance our external lives. There is always so much to do, so much to strive for, so much to catch up on, to learn, to experience, to overcome, that we forget about giving time to learn about how to manage and balance our internal lives. We must make time to get to know and cultivate our gut, our subconscious, the inner voice which serves as the source of all motivation.

When talking with friends or family, much of the conversation revolves around attaining goals and aspiring to achieve external coordinates, but seldom does anyone communicate the true reason and purpose for why they want to get there.

Where is the dialogue about who a person is and what it would take to satisfy the emotions which are calling him to pursue certain coordinates and goals?

We can't neglect our inner voice, for it is what keeps us healthy and motivated to manifest our potential.

Our differences in reality, each persons' so-called, "alternate dimension" is essentially made up of the aspects of existence that his or her emotional blueprint embodies. Throughout life, our emotional blueprint continuously broadcasts songs of desire like a radio station from the gut. In response, we pursue what we believe these songs are calling us to do. As we dance to the ballads of our gut, of our emotional blueprint, we can get caught up in the melodies and misplace the message of the song entirely.

Sometimes, as circumstances evolve, songs can change abruptly without our concluding the message we were supposed to receive, or end without giving us closure. The most difficult times are when multiple songs are playing simultaneously and we cannot find the rhythm or tune necessary to choreograph our steps.

To meet the requirements and fulfill the needs necessary to decipher the concert emitting from our emotional blueprint, we must orchestrate a method to all the madness. We must find some sense of order in all the chaos. If we are able to do this, we can dance unhindered to the beautiful symphony of our life.

If we are unable to decipher what our songs are trying to reveal about our potential, about who we are and our purpose, then we get stuck in a repetitive cycle, playing the same song over and over again, chasing a melody or lyric that may be broken or incomplete, and therefore can never be fully understood. If we can't find the rhythm or beat to our own song, then we will shall never dance and move toward our potential.

Playing the same broken song over and over again makes it difficult for a person to grow. For a person to truly grow, evolve and elevate, he or she has to decode his or her emotional blueprint. This is no easy task.

Think of your emotional response to my version of reality and the theoretical versions of reality I used for contrast. If your emotional response to a fictional version of reality was aversion, or perhaps stronger than aversion—maybe, it was anger or disgust—then, you need to ask yourself why your emotions were inclined to rise to that level of repulsion.

Begin decoding who you are and perhaps your aversions can expand or transform into respect, or tolerance at the very least.

Maps

People enjoy trying to map out their lives. People want to collect achievements, milestones, and landmarks, such as: a beloved partner, perhaps a family, career, house, car, etc., to reinforce the idea that they are living a successful, complete and purposeful life. Somehow the concept of mapping out one's life by means of external coordinates is accepted as a sort of tradition and is even expected to be somewhat fun, but ultimately necessary to attain success and purpose in life.

What seems to be so difficult that it is almost deemed as being impossible, is mapping out the reasons and emotions behind a person's motivation. A substantial part of getting to know who you are is understanding your emotional blueprint. When you understand why you act or react the way you do to certain ideas, people, circumstances, etc., you will develop a broader insight and relationship with your emotions.

Establishing a relationship with your subconscious (aka your gut, both the engine and the driver behind the wheel of the amazing vehicle you call your body) connects you to the motivations, ambitions, and reasons behind why you do the things you do. When you feel a certain impulse toward a person, situation, or idea, wouldn't it be nice to connect with the underlying reason for why you feel that way?

"To know oneself is to study oneself in action with another

person. Relationship is a process of self–revelation. Relationship is the mirror in which you discover yourself. To be is to be related." – Bruce Lee

Our external relationships mirror the relationship we have with ourselves; it is a window into our emotional blueprint. The way we relate to people, situations, knowledge, etc., is a reflection of how we relate with ourselves. The way we navigate our external journey in life, the way we go about discovering the world, echoes' the way we navigate our emotional quest to attain enlightenment.

Ultimately, we do not just seek a certain level of external success, but a certain level of internal realization as well. Only when one is able to reach the pinnacle of both (external success and internal realization) in relative balance, does one reveal or uncover the power of his or her emotional blueprint and limitless potential.

Emotional Thoughts

Back to the topic of emotions governing thoughts.

I used to be afraid of heights. I would look up at a ladder and my knees would tremble. My stomach would churn at the thought of having to climb anything too tall.

I didn't like this feeling, the feeling of being a prisoner to my aversion to heights. I knew I had to somehow find a way to balance this emotion, so I wouldn't be paralyzed by my phobia. I did not want my fear to conquer me.

I took a trip to Moab, Utah to confront my fear of heights head-on.

It all started when a good friend of mine showed me pictures of the beautiful sandstone cliffs and towers that she used to climb when she lived in Moab. As she was telling me about her grand rock climbing adventures and how she used to scale all these magnificent stone formations in and around Moab, she stopped mid-story to tell me that I would probably make a great rock climber.

When I asked her why she thought that, without hesitation she told me it was because she felt that I had the spirit and personality for it. I think I recall booking a train to Moab, Utah the next day.

The rest is history.

I fell in love with rock climbing and it continues to help me understand my emotional blueprint to this day.

Sometimes all it takes is the faith and encouragement from another to shine the light on the shadows within us.

The insight I gained from rock climbing has helped me understand how my aversion toward something is mostly due to my lack of experience and knowledge of the subject.

Fear can prevent me from forming a healthy relationship with the unknown.

What we don't know may be scary, but if we only participate in what we do know we will never learn more than what we are comfortable with. We will never broaden our understanding of ourselves or of the world. Our aspect will never fully bloom and our emotional blueprint won't have the insight and experience to weave new threads into the web of life and expand the spectrum of existence.

Real growth and self-knowledge comes from exploring those deep, dark, and mysterious places within ourselves.

We need not march into these shadowy spaces with the intention of slaying or destroying some monstrous dragon, but with the intention of accepting, understanding and integrating aspects of ourselves that we have yet to truly reveal and discover.

If we approach anything with the intention of acceptance, then we can begin building a relationship with it. It is the forming of a relationship which starts to build a bridge toward understanding.

Relationships can blossom into revelation.

I didn't get over my fear of heights because I conquered some mountain and climbed up some rocks.

I didn't defeat or slay some internal dragon that represented my fear of heights.

I accepted, understood and integrated my fear of heights.

I pulled the unknown (the subconscious) into the known as part of my conscious self.

I intentionally developed a healthy relationship with my emotional aversion toward heights while giving proper respect to the unfamiliarity, or mystery of it all.

It is hard to explain and difficult to understand if you have never experienced it, but the relationship between what we are doing and why we are doing it is the key to understanding how we can integrate our subconscious into our conscious, so we can elevate and expand beyond our fears.

"Instead of establishing rigid rules and separative thoughts, we should look within ourselves to see where our particular problems lie and our cause of ignorance. You see, ultimately all type of knowledge simply means self-knowledge. You must look for truth yourself and directly experience every minute detail for yourself." –Bruce Lee

When a concept, person or scenario presents itself to you and you feel some form of aversion toward it, it can perhaps be because you cannot identify yourself anywhere within that aspect or structure. Your version of reality and the version of reality you are being presented with don't align. You could say it's a form of cognitive dissonance which stems from emotions. Emotional blueprints are unique, but not separate (just as a lion is unique but not separate from a wildebeest, for predator and prey are tied to each other in the web of life), but you may find that some emotional blueprints are positioned further away from yours than others in the spectrum of existence. Without a relationship, a bridge to tie a distant emotional blueprint to your web of reality, then conflict may arise.

Your world and whatever foreign world you are confronted with collide because a relationship has not yet been established. Relationships form an emotional bridge which connect alternate realities together.

Any concept, person, or scenario that falls too far outside the parameters of your "reality" will be seen as a threat because it is too alien, too dark, too unknown to be trusted.

This isn't a bad thing.

This is good because we need boundaries to keep us safe and healthy. Still, our boundaries cannot be too rigid or we will not be able to expand our potential or allow our emotional blueprint to bloom.

Bridging Politics

In American politics there are a number of parties which represent the morals, ethics, and values of a collective group of people, but it is safe to say that the majority of Americans identify themselves as either a Republican or a Democrat.

There are hardcore Republicans and there are hardcore Democrats.

The far right and the far left.

The further to the right or left you sit on the political spectrum, the harder it is to create an emotional bridge to understand the morals, ethics, and values on the other side of the political spectrum because a relationship has to stretch so far across the ideological platform.

It is the people in the middle of the political spectrum who find it easier to come together and integrate their morals, ethics and values. Emotional blueprints positioned near each other are able to build bridges much faster and easier than emotional blueprints positioned in extreme distance from one another.

No matter where in the spectrum of existence we may fall (extreme right or left for example), relationships between emotional blueprints which are close to one another don't have to span across such a large scope of ideologies; therefore the emotional bridges which connect these closely related emotional blueprints are much easier to build and maintain.

Bridging the Gaps between Us

The same model of distance being relative to the bridging of gaps between emotional blueprints is applicable in bridging the generational age gap of a family, as well as the gaps between a community, nation, or the world, for that matter.

This model is also relevant between the disparity of men and women, the social classes, education, religion, cultures, etc.

Wherever your version of reality lies, be it in the middle or either extreme of any spectrum (social, educational, spiritual, etc.), if you are presented with some other version of reality which rests on the far side of the spectrum in which you exist, it can be more than difficult to relate to and unbelievably hard to integrate.

This most certainly applies to caring for someone who has some form of mental disability or condition, like a person with Alzheimer's, or a toddler. (I am just kidding about the toddler part. That was a joke… kind of.)

If you are a parent, then you can understand the emotional bridge which has to sometimes stretch and span pretty far to understand your kids, especially in the first two years.

Building the relationship, the bond between you and your child is one of the greatest and most fulfilling joys in life, but it is in no way an easy task. The alternate reality a child lives in can sometimes seem like complete nonsense to parents, especially around age two.

Two-year-olds are notorious for being both fun and very difficult at the same time. This is because they are learning to interact with the world, which for them, doesn't have any limitations, definitions, or boundaries yet.

Everything two-year-olds do can seem both amazing and ridiculous at the same time. This is because two-year-olds are still emerging from the infant stage of their lives, where everything is based off very sensitive and intense internal systems. They have not yet learned to identify, understand, and cope with the emotional needs of their bodies.

Hypothalamic Guidance

Infants and toddlers are very hypothalamic. I say this because the hypothalamus is responsible for regulating certain metabolic processes. The hypothalamus is a very important gland. The hypothalamus synthesizes and secretes certain neurohormones which stimulate or inhibit even other hormones. It's all very spectacular, but in short, the hypothalamus regulates hunger, body temperature, fatigue, thirst, circadian rhythms… etc., and when you are very young and new to the world, all these systems seem pretty intense and are hard to manage emotionally.

So, on one hand you have a toddler who lights up when he sees an airplane flying in the sky, or a flower which captivates him for a few seconds, then, all of a sudden, everything falls apart. He starts crying and throwing a tantrum because he just realized, or his body just realized how hungry, thirsty, or tired he is.

A toddler's world is driven by the feelings and emotions which rise from the gut and trigger the hypothalamus in the brain to intervene. The hypothalamus moderates many extreme internal situations so balance can be maintained or restored within the systems of the body.

Again, I say everything stems from the gut because although the hypothalamus is in the brain, it receives messages about metabolic processes, thirst, hunger, body temperature, etc., that arise from the core systems which live in or near the gut.

As a toddler grows into a child, hopefully he is learning to manage and cope with all these intense feelings and emotions so he can "play well with others," so to say. Guiding a child to become a well-balanced and functioning kid who can interact with his environment—with a certain level of respect—is one of the main goals as a parent.

This is why "real" parenting is so important.

The purpose of a parent is to guide his or her child to not give in and act or react out of impulse.

The hardest part of parenting is establishing healthy boundaries and instilling the concept of respect into a child, who all his life has only known the powerful needs and emotions which swirl inside of him; needs and emotions which he is unable to meet or balance himself.

It is this extreme vulnerability which causes him to lash out with intense desperation. He instinctually knows that crying and throwing a tantrum will draw attention to himself. He knows the more fuss he creates the higher his chances are of triggering the helpful response he needs from you to make him feel better and make everything right again.

Chapter 2

Language

Chapter two is all about language. More specifically, how language and emotion are connected. This chapter dives into the origins of language, the first language, the universal language, and the purpose of language.

The First Language

The example of a two-year-old's temper tantrum, an intense display of raw emotion, is one reason that I believe the most basic forms of language were born through emotion.

The outward display and expression of emotion is not a universal phenomenon. Not all living things display or express emotion in a way which is easily perceived and understood.

In general, the more ancient or primal the organism, the fewer emotions they are capable of expressing. Some, like jellyfish, for example, are completely incapable of expressing emotion, at least discernable to us. In fact, jellyfish don't even have brains. Jellyfish are driven by their gut instinct to eat, survive, and proliferate. Mainly, it's species of higher intelligence which are capable of expressing the emotion necessary to produce a discernable form of language.

Just to make myself completely clear, I am talking about the ability to express emotion, specifically, emotional cues conveyed on the face of an animal, or emotional sounds conveyed within a structured system (language). Most, if not all mammals are capable of communicating their feelings through facial gestures or sounds. For example, wolf cubs use their voice to call to their parents when they are hungry and adult wolves snarl and growl to communicate their status in the dominance hierarchy or when they feel threatened.

From my observation, if you subscribe to the version of reality which includes evolution as a scientific truth, the more evolved animals (mainly mammals), have not just a higher level of intellect and capacity for learning, but in almost equal parts, a higher degree of consciousness as well. Within this book we define consciousness as having awareness of one's own existence. There are varying levels of consciousness. Lower forms of consciousness may have the ability to comprehend their own existence, while higher forms of consciousness seem to also display an awareness of the collective existence of all creation. As consciousness elevates even more, conscious beings are able to develop theories pertaining how each creation plays a part (has a specific roll) in the spectrum of existence.

Beings with higher levels of consciousness give rise to more than just the awareness of existence, but a way to communicate and express feelings and emotions: language. The ability to express this awareness through some form of emotional language stems from the ability to grasp and display, to some degree, an understanding of consciousness itself.

The higher the consciousness, the more complex the language. Lower consciousness may produce some sort of communication through body language or some vibrational frequency, while higher consciousness may produce communication through sound in a structured system, facial gestures, or even convey messages through pictures, like hieroglyphs and the written word to convey language.

Elephants, Dolphins and Chimps, Oh My!

Elephants, dolphins and chimps are just a few examples which support my perspective of species with higher levels of consciousness communicating through a more complex and structured language. Elephants are highly social animals who feel a wide range of emotions, including sadness. Elephants mourn their dead, conveying sadness through body language as well as trumpeting and showing feelings of sorrow with their trunks.

Dolphins communicate in a way which can be said to be more effective than human language. Dolphins also seem to project a level of awareness and consciousness which mirrors our own. For example, if you think of the animal kingdom and how much time is allocated for rest, grazing, hunting, etc., dolphins will try to experience joy in just about every aspect of surviving. Play is heavily incorporated into hunting as well as swimming, and when dolphins communicate it's almost as if they're telling jokes, emitting a form of humor and joy which is closer to the expression of a human rather than an animal. Joy can be like a holy quest for humans, while joy is something dolphins just seem to embody, it's basically their essence.

Chimps are almost like very young children. Their display of emotions are so close to our own that some people have studied and lived with these majestic apes as if they were part of a human community.

Evolution and Elevation

Given enough time, evolution creates more and more complex biostructures. The gut, the vertebrae, and the brain are all examples of varying structural complexities within evolutionary physiology. As more complex biostructures are created, evolution, in turn, gives rise to more elevated beings embedded with a wider range of emotions.

In my version of reality, emotions are the gateway to awareness and consciousness (while advanced consciousness gives rise to advanced levels of emotional expression). So, as more complex biostructures are a product of evolution, higher levels of consciousness are a product of elevation with emotion at the center of it all, expanding the spectrum of existence.

I say emotion is at the center of it all because I believe emotion is the force behind both evolution and elevation.

I believe emotion is the reason evolution and elevation exist.

Everything wants to establish a relationship with its environment and relationships are stronger when there's ample emotion to experience this connection. Creatures evolve to produce and create the required bio-structural systems which can hold or house emotion. Once emotion takes root, feelings slowly expand the gut, creating a more complex digestive system which will in turn, require more brain power to operate, and thus a higher level of intellect to manage.

When the mind evolves enough, to the point that the creature becomes aware of its own existence, "BAM": consciousness. Consciousness is born through the meeting or merging of the highly evolved mind and the highly evolved gut by process of elevated emotions which expand the potential, structure, and overall spectrum of existence.

Language, Religion and Emotion

The origin of language is highly debatable; a number of theories exist as to how language came about.

I approach the origin of language in a similar fashion as to how I approach the origin of religion. Like religion, language is developed within a structure which is in tune with the culture of its people. The varying degrees of just our own language, English, supports this. In North America, the West Coast, Midwest, South, and East Coast regions all have distinct accents, with sub-variations among each. There are slang terms that only Californians use while major inner cities have developed a language which has birthed a whole new dictionary of terms called: Ebonics.

I grew up speaking a language other than English.

My other language, which is a Philippine dialect, infuses much more emotion behind most words than does the English language. There are times where a single word in Ilongo used in a certain situation under the right context, can draw out levels of emotion that surpass definition.

Religion does this as well.

For me, religion is a symbol for the assortment of emotions; the array of feelings which elude reason or logic within the constructs of our understanding. Through language and religion (I was raised Roman Catholic, but have not identified as a Catholic for decades) have I cultivated a deeper understanding of what "belief" is.

Those who declare that their religion is the, "one true religion," to me, is like someone declaring that their language is the, "one true language," rejecting all other languages and labeling them as inferior and perhaps even blasphemous.

Understanding more than one language has greatly increased my insight into the emotion and meaning behind words. I can see how the fluency of multiple languages can increase the intellect and emotional knowledge of an individual. I believe the same to be true for the development of spiritual understanding and knowledge of multiple religions.

The Hills are Alive with the Sound of Emotional Music

Perhaps an easier way to look at emotion being at the heart of language and religion, without any comparison to cultures or belief structures, would be to look at a personal pastime of mine: climbing mountains.

In another life I was an avid rock climber.

I've done traditional rock climbing, where I clipped my rope into protective gear as I made my free ascent up a rock formation, and I have also enjoyed old-fashioned mountaineering, using crampons and an ice ax to summit elevations above 14,000 feet.

Some mountains or rock formations have captivated me to such an extent that I was more than compelled to reach their peaks. I became committed to reach the top of some of these crags with such a devotion that I came to almost worship these monumental geological wonders. It was almost as though these cliffs pulled me to them with a magnetic force which I found inescapable. Summiting various peaks of all shapes and sizes in extraordinary locations and under diverse conditions revealed something very important to me.

No matter how much I imagined the summit of some mountain or rock formation would illuminate a different version of the world and grant me some secret of life, or meaning of existence, my eventual arrival at the peak always announced what I already knew to be true deep within me all along. Reaching the top would simply remind me why I climbed the darn thing in the first place; to overcome a worthy and inspirational challenge so I could find my limits, push past them, and discover a little more of myself. Discovering the path up the mountain, in turn, helped me to discover the path within myself, which would eventually help me to reveal the magical views at the top—as well as a more authentic understanding of myself.

When I eventually reached the peak, I was awarded with an elevated perspective of the foreign terrain I just explored. The summit granted me an overview of the strenuous journey I had just accomplished. The path I climbed resonated with me as a reflection of how I had to accept, understand, and integrate some foreign terrain or aspect of myself which allowed me to elevate to the crest of the mountain.

Eventually, after enough adventurous climbs, I came to understand that I would only ever reach the peak of a difficult climb when I was emotionally ready, never any sooner. The process and the journey prepared me emotionally to elevate. When I was finally ready to reach a new level of emotional maturity, I would then be worthy of the summit and the expansive views which only its peak could grant.

The view at the top was always bittersweet, for always there was another summit which called to me from a distance.

A Transcendent Purpose

It is our inner dialogue, our inner language which drives us and motivates us to pursue certain things. You could say that it's a song that never ends. Ultimately, we yearn to connect with ourselves and others and to identify with a higher power, a transcendent purpose which will keep us infinitely motivated to evolve and elevate.

Religion fulfills that desire for many people, but for me, it's just plain and simple: love.

Experts and scholars have been debating and theorizing the origin and reason behind the development of language for a long time.

Again, for me, it's simple.

Language first came about, whenever it came about, in whatever dialect or sound structure it was first uttered, to organize, to grasp, to discover, to understand, to expand and relate to one another the mystery of love. This is why for me, emotion is the origin and the reason behind language.

I also believe emotion to be responsible for the inception of religion, art, music, dance, poetry, etc.—all avenues for the expression of emotion.

The development of the human soul, the human spirit, springs from the well of human emotion. The seat of mankind's creativity and achievements, whether it be for vain ambitions or for altruistic intentions, is derived from emotion and the quest to understand the mystery of love.

Evolution produces more and more complex biostructures which in turn produce more and more elevated levels of consciousness. It is our level of consciousness which holds our species closer to divinity than any other on Earth. It is our elevated understanding and perspective of love which allows us to connect with all of existence.

It is our awareness of our emotions and the desire to connect to and understand the mystery of love which has given birth to language and propelled our advancement as a species.

The Universal Language

If there are still any lingering doubts within you as to the connection between emotion and the advent of language, I ask you to consider a language which has been around since the start of it all, the beginning of time and existence itself.

That language is of course, the universal language of love.

The universal language of love intersects and surrounds everything, binding us all.

No matter what version of love we believe in, perhaps we can all still agree that love is the deepest and purest of emotions that somehow transcends all yet connects everything at the same time.

Chapter 3

Learning

Chapter three delves into emotional learning. Emotions can either block or amplify our ability to learn. To prevent our emotions from blocking our ability to learn, we must master our emotions, for mastering our emotions will allow us to harness our emotional strength.

Emotional Learning

It is through love that we learn.

It is through emotion, the strongest of teachers, that we internalize distinct and powerful experiences into lifelong lessons. An emotion we experience can be so intense in one way or another that it is actually imprinted into our emotional blueprint for future use as a basis for knowledge.

Our emotional blueprint is composed of emotional markers, carved out through our personal experiences, which create a map of how we should act or react in certain situations. To keep us safe, our emotional blueprint creates paths for us to follow that keep us away from emotional triggers which can cause emotional discord in our lives.

Following paths which avoids certain emotional triggers is one way we form habits. The other way we form habits is by pursuing a cycle which consistently rewards us with instant gratification or lures us in emotionally with the idea of pleasure or reward.

Mastering Emotions

If we don't learn to manage our emotions and establish healthy boundaries, our emotional blueprint will control our lives. Our emotional blueprint will become the master plan and the master mind behind all we do. This is the basis for the concept of mastering our emotions, for if we don't master our emotions, they will master us.

The concept of mastering our emotions so that they do not master us has been in use for centuries as part of the foundations of philosophy, early spirituality, religions, martial arts, etc. The aforementioned disciplines are just a few platforms in which the practice of mastering our emotions may allow an individual to achieve a higher level of success in any branch of knowledge; this concept also holds true for the general success one attains in life.

Understanding yourself through mastering your emotions is a teaching which has been passed down through generations and has not only survived, but prevailed as an irrefutable contributor to one's prosperity, even being adopted and applied by modern-day business people.

Basically, mastering our emotions helps us understand ourselves. All mastery comes from a deep understanding of a subject. One could be a master artist, a master chef, or a master warrior. Whatever discipline one chooses to devote themselves to, one must remain balanced. Becoming a master requires a deep and intimate understanding of their craft in a way which integrates the discipline itself into a way of life. Mastery is harmonizing a discipline as part of one's nature. Mastery is a way of life.

To master your emotions you must devote yourself to understanding your feelings. Although this may sound like a serious discipline, your methods should not be too ridged. You must find joy from the practice of understanding yourself. There must be an abundance of love and an endless amount of joy which overflows and spills into all aspects of your life. Find happiness and humor in feeling whatever you feel. Like the dolphin, find joy in experiencing all varieties and extremes of emotion in any and all situations. If you can find the humor and joy in any situation, in any emotion, then you will always be able to find your way back to harmony.

Mastering your emotions is less about taking control and more about understanding where you are within yourself—with what you are feeling and experiencing—so you can proceed with clarity.

At times, emotions can feel dangerous. At times, emotions can get out of control. At times, emotions can seem so unfamiliar that you feel completely lost and confused.

Whatever you feel, whether it be an extreme infatuation or a profound pain, don't limit or suppress what you are feeling. To master your emotions all you have to do is understand why you are feeling the way you are feeling. If you understand why and how you got to the feeling you are experiencing, in whatever level of intensity, then you will know your emotional location in relation to joy. If you know your location in relation to a universal constant (like joy) then you will be able to find a path back to harmony.

You can feel overwhelmed and still have the comfort of knowing you will be safe. You can feel out of control and still be reassured that you will be able to manage. You can feel utterly confused with the knowledge that you will never be lost.

Mastery is also about transformation. A master artist can transform shapes and colors on a canvas into a work of art. A master chef can take basic ingredients and transform them into an extraordinary banquet fit for any celebration. A master of emotions can transform experiences and feelings into the energy which will motivate his meaning and power his purpose.

Emotional Strength

We don't do something because we think it. We do something to satisfy a feeling, an urge—a desire.

More than anything, we are motivated by our emotions.

Laziness is not a byproduct of mental weakness, but the lack of emotional desire. One can accomplish the impossible if he or she is filled with desire and fueled by emotion.

The body follows the mind, but the mind follows the intensity of the emotion. When we are emotionally devoted to a cause, person, or place, then we project value, care and support onto those things. Our effort is greatly maximized.

Emotion over mind and mind over matter.

When emotion dies, motivation dies. When we see an inspiring movie, read an inspirational story, or are part of an influential and encouraging workshop, we come out with high emotions which ramp up our motivation. Without consistent emotional encouragement or the projection of emotional value, our motivation slowly and steadily dwindles. The potential for success and elevation is still there, but the fire, the emotional desire, fades, and thus with it the will to put forth the necessary effort to manifest our potential into reality.

We all dream of achieving our potential. We all want to come to realize our full ability. When we think of the ideal body and the ideal mind, we think of the physical and mental training it will take to attain those attributes, but the true power dwells in—emotional—

training.

More than anything, we need to cultivate emotional endurance; for emotional endurance is the price we pay for life itself.

There is a phenomenon between emotion and next level strength. In the times of the sword and shield it has been said that one warrior fighting for his family and village is worth 10 hired soldiers. When people commit to something with an emotional purpose, as long as they don't submit to the emotion and let it overcome or overwhelm them, then they are able to acquire and embody a form of supreme energy and strength beyond whatever challenge is presented to them.

One becomes a force to be reckoned with. A force of nature.

Stage 2: Summer-Formation-Day-Understanding

In stage two we transition from spring to summer. Stage two is the formation stage where potential manifests into reality. This stage takes place at the peak of day, when the sun is at his brightest. It is during stage two that we shift from accepting where we came from and who we are, to understanding why we are here (connection) and what we are meant to do (love). Sometimes, to come to a greater understanding we must experience loss. Loss can reveal the importance of being seen, being heard, and connecting.

To be who we were meant to be we must also remember to embrace our wildness—our primitive and untamed nature—with full emotional accountability, for when we hold ourselves accountable, the path to love is clear.

Chapter 4

Expression

Chapter four demonstrates how emotions can still be expressed loud and clear—even when a person is blind, non-verbal, and is limited in ambulation. This is a story of how emotion is the basis for our greatest desire: connection.

Nonverbal Emotions

Here I present a story of a boy who I work with that is physically trapped within his body, emended from one of my other books titled: *How to Heal and Connect with Yourself and Others through Emotional Intelligence and Healthy Boundaries*. Even though this boy is nonverbal, he experiences and expresses emotion and the need for connection. Since he cannot see or speak (in a way that you nor I can easily understand), his emotions are often conveyed through dynamic and dramatic methods such as hitting, biting or punching, not unlike the theatrical temper tantrum of a two-year-old trying to convey his or her needs. Due to his conditions, some of his other senses are more developed, and thus, also more sensitive than the average person. His desire for connection is more pronounced because of his inability to connect using the "normal" methods of speech. Still, he is able to connect using sound and touch.

I share this story in hopes you won't become an able-bodied version of the conditions which seem to impede this beautiful boy from achieving the true magnificence and art which dwells within

44

him—within us all. As you read this story, empathize with his situation, apply it to your situation, and contemplate on what may be holding you back from your potential. If you are a fully-functional and capable human being, perhaps you will come to realize that there is nothing preventing you from achieving your goals but the limitations set forth by your own inner voice.

I hope you enjoy.

Emotional Healing and Connection through Sound and Touch

This chapter will be broken into two parts: Emotional Connection through Sound for the Visually Impaired and Emotional Healing through Touch for People with Brain Conditions and Injuries.

Part One: Emotional Connection through Sound for the Visually Impaired

At work, my main charge is a young man with a brain condition who is visually impaired. In this section, I focus on how sound plays an integral role in connecting with and caring for someone who is visually impaired.

Imagine you are deprived of sight, the sense above all other senses that allows you to establish and define who and where you are in relation to your environment.

Just thinking of being denied the ability to see can be very scary. Where darkness breeds uncertainty and fear, light propagates clarity and understanding. One of the scariest notions of being stripped of sight is the amount of uncertainty that would arise in relation to how we see (or don't see) and interact with the world.

Ray Charles

From my understanding, the visually impaired young gentleman I work with lives with limited to almost no sight at all. For anonymity purposes, I will refer to him as Ray Charles, or Ray for short. Ray Charles is also a fitting alias because like Ray, he loves music.

There are a few more things to understand about Ray. He is challenged in more ways than one. Vision isn't the only hurdle he has to overcome. Imagine being predominantly wheelchair-bound, unable to express yourself through language, half your body mostly crippled, dependent on others for essentially everything, having to grapple with a brain condition, and on top of it all, not having the ability to see.

I am not going to sugar-coat anything; Ray's life is hard. His life is hard on him and hard on the people who love and take care of him. Yet, through all the strife, Ray finds real and genuine happiness. One of the two main outlets which give Ray pure joy and a sense of emotional connection is sound.

Sound

Sound is something that perhaps people with intact vision take for granted. Sure, we appreciate certain styles of music and can get irritated by nagging or annoying tones, but because we have sight, we don't need to rely on sound or any of our other senses as much to satiate our appetite for sensory stimulation.

Sound is definitely influential. I haven't met a soul (with unblemished hearing) who doesn't connect in some way to a particular style or genre of music. There are also natural sounds which induce a sense of tranquility and harmony. The sound of a bubbling creek, bugs humming, and birds chirping are just as much music to the ears as any man-made symphony or orchestra.

Vision can disrupt and overpower the tones and melodies which are trying to connect with our emotions. As a grateful person with uncompromised health and fully functional senses, I understand that I get much of my sensory stimulation through sight.

Sight

My surroundings influence my mood and emotions. I am aware that I am constantly taking in and processing my environment. I adjust my thoughts and actions in relation to what my eyes perceive around me.

I believe most people rely heavily on the sense of sight. For me, if I cannot physically see what is happening, then I feel almost incapable of making a decision. I don't know if I should act one way or the other. For the most part, whatever I hear, taste, smell, or even touch only becomes real if I can visually confirm it. Vision validates the data gathered from my other senses.

I have to see it to believe it.

Ray can't see. The sensory data that he gathers do not go through the central confirmation center of sight. His world is not like that of a person who can see. Once sight is taken out of the equation, all of the background sensory stimulation that may have once been taken for granted comes rushing forward.

Time Factor

From my experience with Ray, time is understood in a different way as well. Night isn't necessarily for sleeping and day doesn't imply that one must be awake and active.

Depending on the sensory input, how much stimulation is occurring around him and whether or not he is able to interact with any of it, Ray might decide to sleep. Also, he might just be really tired from not sleeping the night before.

A World Made of Vibrations

Ray is very sensitive to sound. For most of us who can see, the loud clatter and chatter of a busy room can somehow be dulled down. Our vision allows us to focus on a scene, object or task, and drown out all our other senses so we can zero in on what captivates us—like a sniper who is visually focused on his target in the middle of a war zone. Ray doesn't have this ability.

Ray's world is comprised of the commotion of his environment. Sound, not sight, makes up his world.

Have you ever listened to your favorite song while doing chores to help you get into a better mood? Doesn't the rhythm help you get into the groove while you are multitasking? The song helps lift your spirit while simultaneously lightening your work load. It is an amazing phenomenon.

Have you ever listened to that same favorite song when you were free from obligations? Were you able to relax into the beat and align yourself to the harmony with your eyes closed, focusing only on the melodies and lyrics?

For me, when I close my eyes and direct all my attention to the music, the song gains multiple levels of depth and dimension. All of a sudden, every beat, sound and melody of the song becomes much more vivid.

This is what I believe Ray's world is like.

Sound Energy

There is energy behind every sound. When we communicate, our words are heavy with intention. Because we almost always communicate with others who are visually adept, our words are painted with heavy tones to command attention. What we forget, or sometimes don't even take into consideration, is that when we communicate with someone who is visually impaired, those same heavy tones that are necessary to convey wants and needs to someone with sight can be completely overwhelming to someone who cannot see.

Someone who is visually impaired doesn't need to have heavy tones embedded into words to overcompensate for the distraction of vision. The energy behind the voice and the urgency of the intention doesn't need to pierce the ears to penetrate the central confirmation center of sight.

Less is MORE

I have been working with Ray for two years now. It wasn't until my second year that I discovered that gentle words and whispers are far more effective than belting out instructions or showering him with exciting words of encouragement. The instant gratification of seeing that he is accomplishing a task or progressing in some way is nonexistent.

When Ray moves or engages in a physical task, he moves slowly and cautiously. It makes sense that the energy and intent behind any words of encouragement or instruction should correspond to the way Ray interacts with the world.

Sugar Ray Leonard

Despite all of Ray's challenges, he is not a meek-mannered or sensitive person. Ray is a rough-and-tumble kid. He enjoys substantial physical contact, including elbow strikes, head-butts, punching, biting, chin popping, and tickling.

Ray's taste in music is in alignment with his physical preferences. Ray loves hard rock and country music. The way he dances in his wheelchair reminds me of a punk rock mosh pit.

Ray's tough-guy persona is on full display when it comes to

communicating with him. If I ask Ray to do something or tell him that a transition is about to happen in my normal voice, he usually screams and yells and protests by elbow striking, head butting or even punching.

Yummy in the Tummy

One of the biggest hurdles Ray and I had to get over was eating time. If I told him in a normal voice that he had food and his fork or spoon was loaded with yummies, he would yell, cover his mouth and/or push away from the table (most times).

It has only been recently this year that I started to softly and gently whisper that his food was ready. I would then gently place his hand where his food and loaded utensil were and whisper for him to take a bite. I would also allow him to smell hot food for a brief period so he could process the idea of eating. Sometimes he still wasn't sold on the idea of dining. I would then have to hold the spoon or fork under his nose for him to finally take interest in his food.

As often as this technique works, there are still times when there is no getting through to him. No matter what *I* do or try, it all really depends on whether Ray is willing to cooperate, and there are many factors that come into play for him to be ready and willing to participate. For one, Ray's sleeping schedule seems to not be structured in a normal diurnal pattern. Sleep affects mood, appetite, digestion and many other aspects of the human condition.

Ups and Downs

One of the biggest challenges of working with Ray is his massive mood swings. Ray is an amazing human being, and like all amazing humans, he wishes to express himself and to communicate his needs. This is a highly frustrating aspect for Ray and the people who love and care for him.

Ray seems to move in and out of the highly adrenalized mode of fight-or-flight quite often. It is hard to pinpoint the triggers that set him off in one way or the other. The only thing for sure is that when he transitions to an aggressive state, you'd better watch out for your safety as well as his. Ray applies palm strikes to his head and elbow strikes to his chair to release the frustration. It can be intimidating if you are not familiar it.

The Sound of Music

Although whispering and gentle words might not always work, there is something that has never failed to get him to transition or shift away from anger and frustration. Music. The sound of music has always calmed Ray down and put him in a better place emotionally and, thus, mentally.

There really is such a thing as good vibrations.

Inter-Galactic Planetary, Planetary Inter-Galactic

From my observations, Ray MOVES through music. I'm not talking about physically moving, like dancing or grooving, (although he does, and quite well actually) but something far deeper. This is perhaps an incredulous theory, but because Ray can't get up and physically explore the world around him, I believe music helps him to move and travel in (and out of) his mind in a sort of "out of body, other dimension or alternate reality" sort of experience.

Have you ever had a really stimulating conversation with someone, and before you knew it, it felt like neither of you was on planet Earth anymore? Like the connection was so authentic and genuine that everything else seemed to get canceled out, and it was just the two of you, and both of you were somehow transported to another realm?

It is a wondrous experience.

51

Another example is if you have ever been to an amazing concert. When the band is in perfect sync, the atmosphere is brimming with positive vibrations, the acoustics are crisp and everything feels in perfect harmony, then magic just sort of happens. When the conditions are just right, the sound and melodies travel through you and sweep you away. The music grabs your soul and whisks you to a place of pure bliss.

This can be hard to imagine if you have never experienced either of these phenomena, but I swear I see it happening when Ray is fully immersed in the sound of music.

Go Big or Go Home

The other reason I believe that Ray uses sound to move and travel in a sort of "out of body experience" is because everything about him seems to be to the extreme. Rarely is Ray in a place of balance. Even when he is, he doesn't stay there for long. When I think of Ray, he is either in the extreme mode of fight-or-flight, or in a euphoric state of singing and rocking-out to his music.

If Ray lives in extremes, then it seems plausible to me that his transition from an aggressive fight-or-flight condition wouldn't stop at a place of mundane melancholy. His emotional pendulum doesn't swing all the way to pandemonium, only to swing back down and stop midway to rest calmly in the middle. No, it continues to swing with massive and substantial force all the way to the other extreme, topping out to what seems to me like an out-of-body, euphoric experience.

Feelings, Nothing more than Feelings

What I have come to understand from my experiences with Ray is that our emotions influence our mental state far more than our mental state influences our emotions.

It is less of "what we see we believe" and more of "what we feel we believe."

Even though I have perfect vision, I have come to acknowledge and understand that my mental state (or mood) is governed by the EMOTIONAL reactions I allow to arise in relevance to the situations and circumstances I am confronted with.

I may be witnessing or watching something beautiful, but if my emotions are withdrawn, sad, or anxious, then I am unable to fully appreciate any of the wonders of life that are blooming all around me.

My days with Ray involve helping him to get through and balance his emotions. Gentle words and whispers help, and music is the default go-to when nothing else seems to work, but somehow, if all else fails, then I bring out the big guns: touch.

Part Two: Emotional Healing through Touch for People with Brain Conditions and Injuries

The second outlet that gives Ray pure joy and emotional healing is touch.

As violent as Ray can be, he is a sucker for holding hands. If you give Ray your hand he is like a kitten being scratched behind the ears. He can't get enough of it. Almost immediately, Ray begins to sing and manipulate your hand in his so he can get you to rub his sternum. Ray loves chest rubs. He also enjoys beating his chest like Tarzan with your hand in his, though he only does this if he has someone's hand in his hand.

Recognition

At times, I wonder if it is some sort of greeting ceremony. When he takes my hand and positions it just right in his to enable him to rub my hand on his chest, it almost seems as if he is trying to communicate on a deeper level. Sort of like, "Hi, this hand is you. I feel you, I acknowledge you." Then, when he repositions my hand in his and beats his chest, it is sort of like he is saying, "This is me... this is where I am. Can you feel me? Can you see me? I am right here."

It is completely and utterly endearing.

Membrane

Ray has a brain condition. This is what I believe hinders him from learning language. The inability to communicate, more than anything, seems to be the main cause of his frustration and anger.

I interpret Ray's emotional outbursts as a by-product or side effect of the emotional pain that must build up from his inability to communicate his wants and needs effectively.

Significance

Self-expression is deeply rooted in how we identify ourselves as individuals. Language is the main and preferred method we use to convey who we are and what we stand for. There are other methods for sure. Music is one of them. Another is dance, and of course there is art... but all these other forms of self-expression are processed and understood through language.

Since Ray cannot see or verbally communicate, touch is his outlet for self-expression and communication.

Helping Hand

When he grabs ahold of someone's hand, Ray begins the process of emotional healing. You can see his face light up like a kid on Christmas morning. What's more, Ray has a genuine expression of joy that radiates throughout his body.

It doesn't matter what mood Ray was in before he had your hand. Once your hand is firmly in his, he becomes a happier, healthier person. Now, this can seem great, and it is utterly amazing for the most part, but there is a catch.

The Song that Never Ends

Have you ever started a conversation with someone who doesn't know when or how to stop talking? You don't want to be rude, but at the same time you are getting exhausted and overwhelmed by the conversation and his incessant chatter. Even when you flat out tell him you have to go, he keeps talking, like your time or obligations don't matter.

That is definitely what touch is like with Ray. When you give him your hand, you have just committed to a one-way conversation that becomes exhausting, is hard to break, and won't usually end well. Once the hand is gone, that emotional pendulum tends to swing the other way, fast and hard.

I get it, though. Not being able to communicate on the same platform (sight and language) utilized by everyone else must be difficult. Emotional outburst or not, it is good to know that emotional healing is just a touch away.

Cues

Ray is cognitive enough to understand simple commands and physical cues.

Ray can't toilet himself, nor does he know when he needs to go to the bathroom. So when Ray needs to be changed, we request his assistance to help him stand from his wheelchair. Although we talk him through the process, he understands that the simple nonverbal cue of touching his back and putting an arm under his shoulder is a prompt for him to push up from the chair and stand.

Ray is not able to stand without assistance. For this reason, there are always two people helping to change him. Ray also knows to hold onto a rail in the bathroom to help orient and stabilize himself while his brief is being changed.

Again, placing Ray's hand to show him where his food or drink is, is enough of a nonverbal prompt for him to understand that it is time to eat. Ray even understands that after he gets out of his gait trainer (a walking device that he uses to walk around on his own) he has to step backward to sit down in his wheelchair.

All this may sound like there is a platform for a good amount of improvement to be made (and there is definitely effort being put forth and goals in place to strive for), but the most difficult aspect in making any progress is understanding what motivates him, and how to get and keep him in an emotional space that allows his mind to learn and absorb what we are trying to teach him.

If someone is overly distracted, too emotional or just plain unwilling to learn, then he will not learn.

I am what I am and that's all that I am

Ray's emotional pendulum swings from one extreme to the other so frequently that it is hard to capture that brief window where he isn't too far into in one emotional state to work with and teach.

I don't have an answer. Whatever the solution is, it is elusive to me and everyone else who loves, cares, and works with him. I don't want this to turn into a "How can we save Ray from his emotional mood swings" and get him to follow and fit some configuration of how we would want him to behave, interact, and learn.

Ray is just fine. Ray has enough problems. We don't need to turn him into one of us; one who believes that there is an answer for every problem and that following rules, etiquettes, and some made-up recipe for life is the only way a person will be complete and happy.

Ray is who he is. The question is, can you and I accept that?

99 Problems

The truth of the matter is that Ray doesn't even know or acknowledge that there is a problem. When he can't express himself or communicate his needs, he gets frustrated and angry. When he experiences emotional healing through touch or emotional connection through sound, he is in heaven. The moments in between are insignificant to him because there is not enough feeling or emotion dwelling there.

Getting high on emotions can feel liberating and freeing. Coming down from that high can leave one feeling empty and alone. The struggle for Ray is that when he isn't distracted by some emotion or feeling he is forced to reflect, face and deal with his current situation. I don't know about you, but to me that sounds boring and not fun.

Learning the Hard Way

It's a similar story for the vast majority of us. Most people, (myself included at times) can't handle the truth of our predicaments. Even when everything is in balance and going well, I believe many of us, for some reason, panic. We look for the nearest distraction that will help us avoid confronting the real issues we need to acknowledge to heal.

It seems that we would rather choose to self-destruct in some way rather than to admit there is an obstacle we need to overcome. Perhaps harmony requires too much effort. Maybe emotional balance feels too elusive and too much like a fairy tale, or it may be that it's just too scary to live without any drama.

Either way, I believe this is why it takes so long for so many of us to learn. We are too busy immersed in whatever chaos we put ourselves into, too addicted to the way we want things to be, and too used to the pain of not having our way, that we are unable to shift away from it. Ray is just a raw embodiment and reflection of how most of us live our lives.

The real lesson to take away from all this is that shifting from one extreme to the other will get you nowhere.

Chasing Emotions

I understand what Ray is doing. He is chasing a feeling in a way similar to how an addict chases his next fix. The problem is that replacing one emotion with a different emotion is not always the best fix. Swapping one emotion for another can hinder our ability to process our feelings so we can truly heal. Once we get the emotional closure we need and complete the cycle, we are then able to learn and grow.

Contrary to most of our beliefs, we don't need an emotional fix or some ultimate experience to move on from unhealthy or out-of-balance emotions. Once we decide to accept, understand and integrate any extreme feeling that nudges our emotional pendulum out of balance, we can begin to gain a sense of clarity that will allow us the grace to move through and with whatever difficulty we are facing.

The only way that will happen, though, is if we move toward our problem(s) with courage and compassion. When we decide to put effort into understanding the things that we are opposed to, the things that are causing us pain, we create a bridge between who we were and who we are becoming.

Growth and elevation are about merging and bridging gaps. The clarity necessary to build that bridge resides at the center of all extremes. The good life materializes when our emotions don't fluctuate so wildly. Swinging that emotional pendulum to some excessive feeling to mask or replace another emotion or problem just lengthens and complicates the process of emotional healing.

Extreme Love (Detour from Ray)

It's sort of like when you fall in love with someone. Love takes you to the ultimate extreme of emotions. Love takes over so supremely that you don't even see the person you adore the way he/she really is.

When you are in love, you see your beloved the way you want him/her to be, not for whom he/she really is. Love hurts because when in-love's façade starts to wear off and finally fades away, you are left with a person you don't even recognize because you never got to know him/her past the infatuation that pulled you toward him/her.

Thesis, Anti-Thesis and Synthesis

Love is like a thesis; an idea or theory that you want to prove. People tend to want others to prove their devotion to them. Heartbreak is the anti-thesis, all the stuff that you don't understand, like, or just didn't expect. Heartbreak is the other side of love.

True love exists in the synthesis.

The synthesis is the merging of the two. When love and heartbreak—thesis and anti-thesis—come together and merge, the whole picture can be put together. The synthesis of the two complements is where learning, elevation, and growth live. The further off you are in any one direction, the further off you are from the truth.

I have come to understand that love encompasses everything and true love resides in the integration of it all.

Back to Ray Charles

If I couldn't see, communicate or ambulate by myself, I would want to feel something more than what would seem as random stimulation as well. I don't know how else I would know I was connected to the world in a meaningful way. The concepts of progress, achievement, behavior, good, bad, right and wrong... these are all abstract concepts and simply inconsequential to Ray.

Ray may not have the ability to see, but he also doesn't get caught up chasing material things or ideas that have no real value or relevance to what comprises a good and healthy life.

What Ray connects with is sound and touch. When he is listening to music or is gripping a person's hand, he is complete, he is happy. Is there so much more that he needs to learn? Or, is he teaching something more profound to us?

The Takeaway

For me, what I take from my experiences with Ray is that when all the excess in life is stripped away, when the fancy nonsense that everyone can get so caught up in is torn down, and the illusion of problems that prevent us from moving forward is finally unveiled, what it all boils down to is emotional connection and healing through sound and touch.

I think one half of the lesson is that we all love and appreciate kind, loving and encouraging words. They are music to our ears.

The other half of it is physical touch. I believe humans crave physical connection and compassion like our stomachs crave food. Sometimes we are starved for it. A hug and a compassionate hand can be just as potent as an actual medicine for healing can be.

Ray's world is fraught with overwhelming challenges. In a different way, my world can at times seem just as challenging and overwhelming, but it is good to know that warm words and a warm touch can help it all make sense, and when I am around loving friends and family... it does.

Accept, Understand and Integrate

Thesis, anti-thesis and synthesis.

Each of the stories in this book highlight a similar message, a common thread that weaves through every allegory. That thread or theme is that we all seek connection. Everyone wishes to be a part of a genuine relationship based on acceptance, understanding and integration.

We all wish at times to lead. Other times we wish to be led. Each of us wants to influence and to be influenced. The caveat is that no one wants to be told when to do something or how to be affected by it.

We all need and require the liberty to process new information and experiences with a certain amount of grace and guidance to grow.

A Horse to Water

The old adage that you can lead a horse to water but you can't make him drink applies to every situation and scenario in this book.

The horse might not be ready to drink, or the horse may just flat out not want to drink. Either way, the horse will not drink, no matter how much you whisper, yell, command, or plead. It is never *you* that eventually gets the horse to drink, it's the horse.

If you really believe the horse needs water and that drinking is the best thing for him, then perhaps building a bond and relationship with the horse can implement a stronger influence. The lesson to remember is that even in a good and healthy relationship, no one wants to be manipulated or coaxed to do something he does not want to do.

Just because we believe something to be right because it has worked for us and resonates with whomever we believe we are, doesn't mean that it is right or will even work for someone else.

Morals and Ethics

This is the difference between morals and ethics. Many people get them confused. Morals are an individual's own principles regarding right and wrong. Many times we think we are helping by pushing our morals onto others.

Just as a successful businessman who didn't go to college shouldn't push others to drop out of school, a scholarly teacher shouldn't discourage a budding entrepreneur from leaving academia to follow his dream.

We each have our own path.

Ethics refer to a way of being from an external source. Ethics are not the way you interpret what is right or some personal code you live by. Basically, ethics follow the golden rule: Treat others as you would like to be treated, or, do nothing to others you would not have done to you.

Swimming against the Current

As far as the horse situation goes, if drinking water is still what is best and necessary, perhaps you can guide him to drink by running him through a field. Exercise always builds up a thirst. If that doesn't work, maybe a song near the river-bank will put him at ease enough to take a sip. If that still fails, then you can try brushing him near the water until he feels relaxed enough to drink.

If nothing works, then it may be time to stop putting so much effort into trying to get another to do something you want him to do, and let him find his own way. I think the horse is smart enough not to die of thirst and will drink when he is good and ready.

Side by Side

There is a lot more patience, effort, creativity and humility involved in this method, but it makes all the difference between an influential and inspiring leader and a tyrannical dictator.

Everyone wants companionship. Everyone seeks a connection. We all desire genuine relationships. No one wants to be ruled.

Sometimes the best help is just standing next to someone, not behind or in front, just shoulder to shoulder.

Reflection

As you can see, even in this story, though the boy is nonverbal, he still has quite a language. His inner voice is loud and strong. With all that is going against him, he still manages to feel and express the emotions that he experiences in the most potent ways he is capable of.

Chapter 5

Loss of Language

Chapter five is about losing and finding ourselves. Throughout life we cycle back and forth from being lost to being found. This chapter talks about some ways we can lose, find, and strengthen our inner voice. This chapter touches on emotional accountability and how emotional maturity can reveal a path to love.

Loss of Language by Suppressing Emotions

Physical restrictions, diagnoses and conditions aside, what has happened to the people who seem to have lost their voices?

Most of the time it isn't physical or bio-structural conditions which prevent people from expressing their emotions and cultivating their inner voices. It is the suppression of their emotions.

Why would anyone suppress their emotions to the point that their inner voice is compromised?

The culprit or catalyst for this "depression" in emotion can be any form of trauma. Still, however valid the trauma was which caused a sinking of one's confidence, it should not be used to justify a victim mentality. When one allows himself to become a victim, his inner voice hides behind the trauma which obstructs emotional growth. His cycle of elevation becomes blocked and his energies (emotions) become unbalanced due to the lack of confidence he has in expressing his creative value. The inability to create keeps him lost and adrift in an emotional state.

Our emotional cycle, the process of transforming thoughts, ideas, and potential into reality, is how one develops the confidence necessary to enrich, nurture, and promote one's inner voice. In turn, it is one's inner voice which encourages the elevation of possibility and potential in oneself. Through the continued cycle of creativity, moving or flowing without obstruction into formation and manifestation, do we gain the wisdom, courage, and power to break through our perceived limitations and reach into the realm of limitless potential within us.

If our emotions have limited or no outlet for expression, then our emotions build up and swell inside us like an inflamed infection. Without an outlet for emotions to continue flowing through their cycle, they get stuck, causing an increased sensitivity to any and all stimuli. This increased sensitivity to stimuli can cause us to lash out in pain, anger, or frustration—or worse, we can collapse and hide within ourselves until our inner voice becomes an un-seen, unheard and unrecognizable aspect of what it used to be; a ghostly relic of the potential it could be.

Being Seen, being Heard, and Connecting

When we experience trauma in some way, shape, or form, we may feel that the best way to remedy the situation is to hide.

Perhaps the trauma instills in us a feeling of not being good enough. Perhaps we feel intimidated, overwhelmed or oppressed.

Whatever the reason, sometimes we can give in to the idea that being invisible is the best way to solve our problems. Making ourselves unseen to conflict is a simple solution. Being invisible keeps our interactions with whatever the source of our trauma is to a minimal. Our desire is to neither be seen nor heard in the hopes that whatever opposition we are facing will somehow, in some way, disappear.

What we don't realize is that in the process of becoming unseen to conflict, we ourselves become less visible, and thus less relevant to the world because to become less noticeable we need to, in a sense, conceal, and sometimes to an extreme degree, erase the emotions which would draw attention to ourselves. To cope, our inner voice begins to vanish as our own perception of who we are evaporates. While we continue to disappear, the overwhelming conflict we are confronted with continues to manifest, growing ever more formidable as it dominates our world.

This is the victim mentality.

To connect to our inner voice, we must first be seen and be heard—not so much to others as to ourselves. We must acknowledge ourselves into existence (especially in the midst of opposition) and in the face of adversity, not vanish like some specter or phantom.

First, we have to believe that we matter, that we are real, that we are of substance and value. Only then will we be able to connect to our inner voice and develop our emotional language into a powerful source of courage which supports our claim as a being of value who deserves love and is honored with the limitless potential of elevated consciousness.

A strong and vibrant inner voice reinforces the ability to transform potential into reality, the cycle which confirms our existence and declares our meaning to the world.

A powerful inner voice helps us maintain resiliency in the face of adversity and integrates the energy of opposition into a force which expands our influence and boosts our ability to manifest our dreams into reality.

The Wild Edge

To build physical strength, one must stress the muscle. To build mental strength, one must exercise the mind. To build emotional strength, one must experience emotional discomfort.

Opposition builds strength and resiliency.

If an adult tree has been kept sheltered all its life, unexposed to the weather and the elements, it has a much lower chance of surviving when finally transplanted outside.

This can also be noted in wild animals which have been kept in captivity for a prolonged period of time. These animals lose their edge (wildness) along with the instincts and skills necessary for them to survive in the wild.

No matter how civilized we become, we must maintain a healthy relationship and connection to our wildness—the edge which will keep us resilient amidst adversity. For when we encounter adversity, no matter what shape or form it presents itself, we will be held emotionally accountable for our actions, or lack of actions.

We need to exercise our emotions so we can cultivate the emotional intelligence necessary to mature and manage any obstacle which may come our way.

Emotional Accountability

One of the best ways to build emotional intelligence is to take responsibility for our emotions.

People tend to use their emotions as the biggest excuse for why they don't or can't do something. People tend to exploit their feelings as a handicap so they may avoid certain situations. More than anything, people declare something as impossible because of how they feel toward it.

The environment and circumstances usually can't be changed, but the way we respond emotionally is something we can change.

Being held accountable for our emotions is what allows us to accept, understand, and integrate what we are experiencing.

For example, taking out our frustration on our family because we had a bad day doesn't help to heal the pain of whatever caused us to have a bad day. Holding ourselves emotionally accountable for what we are feeling and seeking support from our family (instead of getting frustrated) can help us heal from the actual cause of the bad day.

Projecting blame onto something which happened during the day and becoming frustrated may not solve anything, while taking emotional accountability for our feelings and seeking support may allow us to accept, understand, and integrate whatever trauma we felt so we can grow or elevate from the experience.

Limiting ourselves because of how we feel is the best way to keep the emotions which exemplify joy and love concealed by the emotional illusions which we choose to pursue in exchange of actual joy and love.

Many value "the chase" above all else. Instead of cultivating joy and love, many of us subscribe to the idea that once we rid ourselves of the situation which is causing our emotional distress, we will be able to experience joy and love.

What can be even worse is when we seek instant gratification to dim the pain of emotional distress in our lives. Instant gratification can lead to impulsive tendencies which can unleash addictive behaviors. Addiction is a way to deny ourselves the ability to process our emotions so we don't have to deal with our feelings. By denying our ability to feel altogether, we can eventually become numb to life itself.

Another idea is that only after we acquire something will the gates to joy and love be opened. The notion that we need to reach a certain coordinate to be worthy of love and joy prevents us from ever experiencing true love and joy.

The Path to Love

The path to love and joy is direct.

The gates are always open and we are always worthy.

We are the ones who block the path, who close the gates, who develop our own detours and pursue other roads. We embark on foolhardy quests in search of emotional fulfillment. Instead of fulfillment, these impetuous adventures bear fool's gold. Overcome with golden fever, we can come to gladly accept fool's gold over real gold and chase impulsive emotions to try to fulfill the desire for the real experience we want: joy and love.

Joy and love are our hearts' desires—delicate and dazzling emotions of pure gold.

When we attempt to create a relationship, to connect with another, we seek to bond with someone who we can trust to cherish our most vulnerable and valuable of treasures: our emotions.

It is in relationships which joy and love are found, experienced, and shared.

Stage 3: Fall-Dream-Dusk-Integration

Stage three is the transition from summer to fall. Whatever we have created during the day desires to become something more at dusk. Stage three is about taking everything we have learned through manifesting our potential into reality and allowing it to come undone. It is from the reassembling of these broken pieces that we are able to form a sharper image of the perpetual dream of existence. We must consistently take apart our understanding of things so we may begin to shed ourselves of the outdated doctrines which restrain us from growing into a more relevant skin.

Chapter 6

Cycles and Spectrums of Energy

Chapter six is about taking apart energies and understanding cycles. What is a day, and how can it be both ancient and new? Where does the energy of a star go when it collapses into a black hole? What is light? Many basic concepts will be broken apart to be put back together in ways which should not be taken too literally. All ancient peoples have stories to describe the origins of the Earth, the heavens, and of life itself. Though some origin stories may seem more like a fairy tale than others, there is but a beautiful and creative truth which prevails. So, let us talk about gravity and love, strings of joy, the law of attraction, loneliness, artificial energy, and potential reality. Let us take apart these things and dissect them to find the pieces which can create such wondrous stories.

Ancient and New

The cycle of elevation has been in motion since the beginning of existence.

Ancient magic.

Since the beginning of existence, there have been many rotations in the cycle of elevation. What started with old magic has evolved and elevated, shifted and changed many times over, but has stayed true and authentic to itself.

Similarly, a caterpillar grows and changes into a butterfly, but remains true and authentic to itself.

We grow and change as well. Who we were when we were children differs from who we were as teenagers, which is hopefully lifetimes away from who we become as adults. As adults, we often change yet again if we become parents. Although we may change, evolve and elevate many times over, the core or code of who we are remains resilient and authentic. You see, it's not really that we change, we expand who we are. We grow. We mature.

The code, or DNA of a caterpillar, doesn't change when it undergoes a metamorphosis and transforms into a butterfly. Likewise, our code or DNA doesn't change when we grow and mature into emotionally competent adults. We do not deviate from our emotional blueprint, we build and expand upon it.

Everything is in motion and in sync or alignment with the cycle of elevation.

The grand cycle of the universe and all of existence, where all cycles live, may take eons upon eons to fully mature and begin anew, while in comparison, a miniature cycle, like a human life, mature relatively quickly.

Cycles vary in vibration and duration. There are cycles so small in vibration and duration, like the life of a mayfly (who only lives for about 24 hours), that their miniature ballad goes almost unbeknownst to us. Even if a mayfly were to land on our nose, the vibrational frequency it puts out is so small in comparison to our own, that we may overlook the significance of this tiny creature's contribution to the grand spectrum of life. Then, there are cycles so large, like our sun, or the love we have for another, that their cycle supports our very existence, vibrating at a frequency as grand as life itself (while the duration of their cycles seems to be nothing short of everlasting).

There are cycles of vibration distinct to ways of life which last millions of years, like the Paleocene epoch, which began about 66 million years ago after the extinction of the non-avian dinosaurs and concluded about 56 million years ago when the climate warmed causing yet another mass extinction. The Holocene epoch, which we are currently in right now, began approximately 11,700 years ago as glaciers retreated (though some scientists believe that human impact has brought us into a new epoch informally dubbed the Anthropocene). There are cycles going on all around us, some so tiny that they are microcosms in and of themselves.

The small or short cycles can seem insignificant to us, while others are so immense that we ourselves can seem insignificant. The farther away a cycle is in comparison to our own, whether it is larger or smaller, the less comprehensible or relative it becomes to us in the way we relate to it in our day-to-day lives. For example, an ant is so small that squishing one doesn't seem like it should have any impact on our lives, and compared to us, the Earth seems so grand and full of abundance (relative to where one lives) that she is easily exploited and taken for granted. Our very lives can seem so boundless when we are young that we take our own youth for granted, much to the dismay of old age.

No matter how big or small, whether it is the cycle of a mayfly or the cycle of a star, all cycles are relative and in alignment with the grand cycle of elevation.

The universe has changed massively since its inception.

The universe has expanded, evolved and elevated countless times over but its code, its emotional blueprint, has stayed authentic.

Past eras and epochs, things that once were, will never be as they were again. For example, dinosaurs will never again reign on Earth (well, maybe in the next grand cycle).

Old ways become irrelevant, untrue, and not useful as the cycle of elevation continues to evolve and expand.

Old magic becomes less potent and irrelevant over time due to outdated structures and shifting energy.

Through the grand cycle of elevation, new spells are woven and new magic flows through all subsequent cycles, large and small. These new germinating seeds of potential bring relevance back into the structure and energy of the universe with respect to the mystery of it all.

New magic birthed from the metamorphosis of old magic knits a fresh new perspective into life, replenishing all of existence with a potent enchantment. This is how each day can feel so repetitive yet filled with so much potential and possibility, and how each sunrise is both ancient and new.

Limitless Energy and Immeasurable Emotions

The energies which sustain the life force of the universe are immeasurable and unobservable when it comes to potential and possibility.

The energy which supports and sustains the universe is self-sustaining and infinitely perpetuating. This is possible because the universe is a cycle of transformative energy.

Energy is constantly being processed or transformed through complementary forces. A battery is a good example of energy being released through complementary forces. A battery has polar complements which produce or release energy when a complete circuit is formed. The universe uses complementary energies the likes of which have no limit, through circuits or cycles to generate infinite potential. The grand cycle of the universe is not made up of just one energy which is recycled in an endless circuit, the grand cycle is composed of countless cycles which are transformed over and over into new cycles. Each of these cycles within the grand cycle can expand and give birth to even more cycles, thus expanding the grand cycle in an exponential and infinite way.

The source of this infinite energy is emotion. If you are skeptical, ask yourself, is there a limit or end to how one can experience joy, love, fear, or anger?

Emotion is immeasurable and without end; thus the perfect source of energy to sustain and perpetuate the universe through its endless and everlasting grand cycle of existence.

It is through the revelation of emotion as the purest form of energy that I have come to understand a fundamental truth. This truth is that opposites do not exist and the concept of separate states is an illusion.

You may have a difficult time with what was just said.

The concept of opposites and separate states is what we learned at a very young age to help us define ourselves and our place in the world. Opposites played a huge role in our ability to understand safety, boundaries, respect, and physical reactions. We needed the concept of opposites to help cultivate the methodical and logical aspects of ourselves which complement our own emotional blueprint. Hopefully, the concept of opposites will have served its purpose by the time we reach adulthood.

The Tree of Life

When I was young, I remember looking at trees and believing them to be separate from each other as well as all the things around them. As I grew, I learned about the role trees played in oxygen and atmospheric production, as well as some of the cycles which affected them (like the seasons and the water cycle), but I still perceived trees to be separate from everything else. A tree was a tree, an insect was an insect, a bird was a bird, and so on and so forth.

As I matured even more, I began to understand the connections between all the things I once saw as separate. A tree started to become more than just a tree, it was a link to so many other creations and cycles. I saw how the branches and leaves extended toward the sky, absorbing and transforming the light and energy of the sun into a new form of energy which was used to sustain itself. I saw the shade it provided to the creatures of the Earth. I saw the insects and animals who adopted it as their home. I saw the food it bore and the varying levels of habitat it created from its canopy to its roots. A tree reached for the heavens while also tunneling deep into the ground, holding the Earth together.

I kept growing, and as I did, I learned that trees also communicate. Through root and mycelium systems, a tree can share a vast amount of plant knowledge. How could this be? A tree wasn't just a tree to me anymore. A tree was everything. A tree supported and affected so many creatures and systems, it reached into so many cycles and realms that my image of it started to merge with everything else. The definition I once had of a tree began to blur and blend in with its surroundings. Not to mention, there was now evidence to support that a tree could actually communicate with other living things.

From this expanded view I was awakened and amazed to the connection which we all share with everything else. From this enlightened perspective I had to figure out how to apply my new found understanding of what a tree was. To do that, I had to make my way back through all the exceptional aspects which made up a tree until it became just a tree again.

Don't get me wrong, I still hold all trees with a very high regard. My respect for trees and all of creation has expanded immensely. It's just that my perspective has also grown and matured. Now, when I see a tree, I see her magic, I see her beauty, I see her stretching and expanding into the cycles and realms of all of creation and existence, but I also see just a tree.

The concept of a tree expanding into all things while still remaining just a tree can be applied to how we view ourselves.

We are not just human, but spiritual beings who seek out the kind of relationships which will allow us to understand the connection we share with all of creation. As we grow and spread into other realms like a tree, we will reveal our purpose. We will find peace in the knowledge of our role, our connection, and our meaning in the vast spectrum of existence. We will expand from the physical and logical world to the realm of emotion and spirit, just to make our way back again as enlightened beings who are able to transform potential into reality.

Our source of power comes from being deeply planted in both the physical and spiritual world. We are more than just human, but divinely human. We are logic and emotion. When we are able to harness the energy created by the dynamic forces of our complex (the complements we are composed of) in relative harmony, we reveal our emotional blueprint and unite with the source of our divinity.

Once we have matured and reached a level of logic which brings a certain level of balance to our emotions (emotional intelligence), then the concept of opposites can become flexible and even transform, or grow into a new concept altogether. Any growth or transformation must be done with respect to the health of our boundaries. So, if this is something you are not yet ready for, please feel free to ease into this next section or perhaps even skip it until you are ready.

Opposites to Complements

For me, the concept of opposites and separate states expanded and evolved into the concept of complementary forces.

Black and white, up and down, good and evil, and life and death are generally categorized as opposites. These so-called separate states help us navigate our immediate environment, but when we expand our very focused and narrow view of life, what happens to these concepts?

For example, imagine you are an astronaut exploring some blank stretch of space, light years away from any star or planet. In such a desolate place, how would you discern which way is up, and which way is down? Do the concepts of up and down even exist anymore?

The colors black and white are generally perceived to be opposites, but the answer on whether either is even a color would vary depending on who you ask. A physicist might say black is the absence of color and white is the blending of all colors, while a chemist might say white is the absence of color while black is a color, a color created by combining pigments or molecular coloring agents of the three primary colors. Then, there's the perception of black and white through the reflection of light. White becomes a color again because white is a reflection of all colors while black absorbs all colors and doesn't reflect any light back. Whether black and white are opposites can seem irrelevant when there is a debate on whether either is even a color. From my perspective, black and white are complements to the color spectrum of light.

Good and evil are perceptions. Before the United States, back when North America was considered "The New World," Manifest Destiny was perceived as good. The conquest of the West in the eyes of the settlers was a divine right bestowed upon them by their God. Reaching the West and taming the land through the domination or eradication of the native people was considered a holy quest for some American settlers. Comparatively speaking, Manifest Destiny was pure evil for the native tribes whose lands, lives, and cultures were wiped out in the process. What is good and what is evil are perceptions of the individual. For me, the complementary energies of good and evil must be balanced to achieve peace.

Life and death are considered to be opposites and separate states. Most of us see life as a finite line of time, yet, the cosmos show us there are no finite lines to be found anywhere. Everything is cyclical. Day turns to night which transforms into another new day, seasons turn and change in a cycle, and even our measure of time is based on the rotation and orbit of the Earth around the Sun. So, why then is life perceived by so many to be an isolated miracle, a single state which is separate from all the cycles of the universe? Through the revelation of emotion as energy, life and death are not opposite or separate states. Life and death form a circuit just like any other cycle. The boundaries which define you will grow and expand like all things. Your physical limitations will eventually extend beyond the bond which holds your flesh and spirit together, to a stage where you will merge and dissolve into the very fabric of existence itself, only to be reborn with a new potential. Like everything else, Life and death are complements which rotate in alignment with the grand cycle of existence.

Common Thread

Rather than "this" defining "that" or "this" opposing "that" we should ask what "this" is in relation to "that," for everything is connected by a fundamental force, a dynamic string of energy which is woven through everything. This common thread of energy ties everything together to demonstrate that there really is no such thing as opposites, just a fundamental force of complements which pull some things together while pushing others apart, only to come back together again in an endless cycle of good and evil, black and white, up and down, and life and death.

Whatever concept we embrace of opposites or separate states, whether it is fear as the opposite of love (for some, fear may not be the opposite of love), or anger as the opposite of joy (again, anger doesn't have to be your definition as the opposite of joy), they are all illusions which we ignorantly adopt and project onto our version of reality. These illusions restrict a more authentic understanding of energy and emotion.

To me, the energy, the common thread which is woven into everything is joy.

To me, the energy, the cycle of pulling and pushing which holds everything together is love.

Magnetic Force

Complements are like magnets.

Complements pull and push one another like two magnets. The magnets spin and orbit one another in a perpetual dance as each tries to connect with their complementary half. When the sides which complement each other are face to face, they are pulled together. When the sides which are similar to each other are face to face, they are pushed apart. One aspect pulls while the other pushes. The field between these two dancing complements is set ablaze with electrifying and living chemistry.

Joy.

What is born from this dazzling and dynamic relationship is a possibility of existence, a spectrum of reality composed of the energy between these two aspects. Every reality born from the dynamic relationship of complements gives birth to a reality which is not singularly composed of just one aspect, but a varied combination of both aspects. Every reality is actually a spectrum which spans the dynamic relationship of two complements. Everything, from a mayfly to a star, is like a magnet dancing in search for its complement. We all seek the kind of relationship capable of creating a beautiful and new version of reality composed of the complementary parts of who we are.

Love.

It is between the extreme aspects of complements that reality is born. The formation of one reality awakens its counterpart and the creation of its complementary reality, which in turn gives birth to yet another reality, and its complement, and so on and so forth. A single reality (life, or existence in any form) created from complements (black and white, masculine and feminine, good and evil) can give birth to the countless cycles and complements which make up the grand cycle of the entire universe.

It don't matter if your Black or White

As in the perception of colors example, black is said to absorb all light (thus making it not a color), while the color white reflects all colors, creating a complement (whether either is a color is irrelevant to me). Without complements there would be no balance.

If black were absent, then the energy of white light would penetrate every corner of the universe. The cycle of day and night would not exist. Without night to complement and balance day there would be no rest. Without day to complement and balance night there would be no action.

If day were perpetual, there would be no dusk, no breaking down the day so we could dream of something more. If night were perpetual, there would be no dawn, no potential released to form a new version of existence because all would remain trapped in the abyss of darkness.

If there were no white to reflect and spread the spectrum of light into the universe then the blackness of night would eventually consume all possibility of life.

While perpetual light would generate a bleak and sterile universe, perpetual darkness would consume existence itself.

Emotions like fear and anger are complements to emotions like love and joy, their energies are just represented as extreme aspects on the emotional spectrum, or spectrum of existence, just as black and white represent extreme aspects in the spectrum of color.

Like the color (or non-color) black, fear and anger are sustained by consuming the energy of the universe, while emotions like joy and love are like the color white, producing and reflecting energy into the universe.

Emotional Digestion

Though joy and love may sound good and fear and anger bad, they are both necessary to create the potential for life. We humans process fear and anger in much of the same way we process food.

When we eat, we break down the food so our body can assimilate nutrients to use as energy. This is the purpose of digestion. We then use this energy (or potential) to manifest or create our physical desires. Our ability to transform physical matter (food) into energy, paired with the freedom to use that energy to manifest any desire we wish into physical form, is a testament to our divinity. Whatever we create, whatever we manifest into existence completes the circuit or cycle of energy which began within our digestive system or gut.

What we manifest from the energy which was transformed from the food (matter) we broke down is a form of karma. We are vessels which process, transform and project energy into whatever we do. This is why taking some of the energy which was so graciously given to us by the food we consumed, and giving it back to the land by cultivating and tending to the Earth, who provides us with all the nourishment we ever need, is so fulfilling and rejuvenating.

We are natural-born stewards of this planet.

This is why gardening is so healing; it connects us with the source of energy we use to make our dreams come true.

Again, we digest more than just food.

If the color (or non-color) black absorbs light energy, what happens to all the light energy? The light energy doesn't just disappear. Black is kind of like the gut, the digestive system of the universe—as black absorbs all wavelengths of light and converts or transforms light into heat energy. With the right conditions, heated elements will glow producing light. This glowing light transmits and reflects the newly processed potential energy back out into the universe. Black absorbs and transforms energy while white beams and reflects energy. Emotions like fear and anger absorb and transform energy while emotions like joy and love radiate and reflect energy.

When we experience a feeling or an emotion, we break it down so that we can understand it. Once we are better able to understand our feelings and emotions, we can then uptake or incorporate them into our lives. This process of emotional digestion (transformation) allows us to expand our knowledge so we may form healthier boundaries. The night helps us to absorb our emotions. We sleep at night to help us reset all the emotions we experienced during the day. A good night sleep is necessary to absorb, process and transform our emotions into knowledge and understanding. Ultimately, all knowledge is self-knowledge and all understanding cultivates a deeper understanding of ones' self.

The breaking down (understanding) and uptake (integration) of our emotions also supply us with the energy needed to increase our potential. It is through the emotional digestion (transformation) of fear and anger that we are able to come to experience a new level of joy and love. We need to process or transform what we don't know or understand, the shadowy aspects of ourselves and "the mystery" into new potential, so we may experience and expand upon the transcendent and self-actualized energies of joy and love. There is no good or evil, there are no opposites or separate states, only the complementary energies which perpetuate growth, evolution, and elevation.

It is through the process of digesting and transforming emotions into new potential that we align ourselves with the cycle of elevation. This process also sustains the energy of the universe itself. One way the universe transforms itself is through the digestion of energy through a collapsing star.

Black Hole Sun

Before we are able to understand what we are feeling, before we digest our emotions, we are in conflict with whatever we are experiencing.

If we are unable to convert and process feelings like fear and anger, then our worries and aggravations will intensify, consuming our emotions and shrouding our logic in a dark cloak. Our experiences are mostly just a projection of how we are feeling. We must remember that we live in our own altered and alternate realities which are produced and influenced by the perceptions and perspectives of our own undigested emotions. We need to digest and transform our feelings so we can expand from emotions like fear and anger and fully experience our reality, as well as the shared reality which makes up the grand spectrum of existence.

Through "emotional digestion" love and fear transform from opposites back into the complements they truly are (and always have been) which sustain, perpetuate and promote the evolution and elevation of each other.

Again, the universe does this as well.

A black hole is the complement to the sun, as fear is the complement to love. A black hole processes energies similar to fear and anger. Like fear and anger, black holes consume energy.

Everything has a price and the price tends to be paid in the currency of equivalent energies or emotions (every action has an equal and opposite reaction). These transactions move in cycles.

The sun provides light and energy for the potential of life and creation to exist. When a sun, a star, dies, (if it is big enough) it collapses and forms a black hole. It is part of the cycle. The energy the star produced and provided to the universe in our dimension is taken back and recycled. For on the other side of the black hole is a new star, a new sun providing light and potential to another solar system, in a sister dimension, where its light may shine in a completely new way.

The new star in this sister dimension may be subject to new dynamics which range from slightly different to dramatically different in comparison to the dimension it came from.

For this is how the cycle of elevation works. Everything in the multi-verse is moving in sync with the cycles. The cycles bring about growth, change, evolution and elevation.

The cycle of processing emotions (which is the force behind energy) is always shifting and cycling back and forth, journeying between one extreme to another within the spectrums of existence. Cycles push the extremes of all aspects, expanding the boundaries of existence ever further.

Behind our sun, in another dimension, is a black hole—a black hole which is consuming the energy which was at one time provided to our sister dimension, and transforming this energy into a new potential, giving life to our world in this dimension.

Through a cosmic digestion process, this dark energy, similar to fear and anger, is transformed into something beautiful, something which mirrors joy and love.

Light and gravity.

Light and gravity radiate the gift of potential, the gift of life within its radius of influence.

Joy is light, the light of life in the universe. Love is gravity, the force which connects and holds everything together.

Light

The structure of light consists of particles (structure will be expanded upon in later chapters), but the frequency of light consists of waves.

Waves = energy, energy = emotion.

The spectrum of color in light represents the spectrum of emotion. The wave frequency, or intensity, is in direct correlation with the type of emotion being transmitted. The visible spectrum of light is in relation to the emotions we experience and understand.

The invisible spectrum which extends toward violet into ultraviolet vibrates with such a high frequency that we are not yet able to process it. This is the reason ultraviolet light is harmful to most, if not all organic structures. Plants have even developed a system to block or filter out UV light.

The invisible spectrum which extends toward red, into infrared is associated with lower-frequency waves. Not much can grow or survive in this spectrum because there is not enough energy or emotion to sustain life.

Low frequency is associated with depression and fear, while high frequency is associated with insanity and madness, for we have yet to elevate enough to integrate and understand it.

Joy encompasses the entire spectrum but is most vibrant and

easiest to identify in relation to our experiences near the center of the spectrum, where light is not only visible, but freely integrated and transformed from potential energy, into usable energy (photosynthesis). From joy everything is created. The spectrum of existence, all aspects and possibilities, the potential to experience any and all emotions, expands and radiates from joy.

High-frequency, or ultraviolet light, takes work end effort to rise to; while low-frequency or infrared light requires little to no effort to sink down into.

Though life may find a way to survive in these extraordinary places, they are still not very welcoming nor conducive to existence. For this reason, most try and live somewhere between ultraviolet and infrared.

No matter what aspect in the emotional spectrum of light one personifies (the idea behind auras and the colors of light associated with them), most seek to express and align themselves with joy (if joy were to be an aura, it would emit a glow of the full spectrum of colors—probably white light—and not just one hue of a color, or an aspect in the spectrum). From joy one can then expand into all spectrums and realms of seen and unseen light unaffected.

Though the high frequency of ultraviolet light may represent a higher understanding of existence, attaining such knowledge doesn't constitute elevation if one neglects to understand the purpose of the lower frequency vibrations of infrared light. Elevation is the expansion of knowledge into all realms of existence (high and low, ultraviolet and infrared, life and death, etc.) in equal parts.

We must acknowledge and respect the validity of it all.

Though the realm of high frequency ultraviolet light may embody divine knowledge, the attainment and understanding of this knowledge is not possible without exploring the low frequency realm of infrared which promotes the will and growth to achieve it.

Low frequency vibrations like infrared light trigger the will to survive.

Where there's a will there's a way. Hence the term "survival of the fittest." This is how and why opposition builds stronger components. Whether it's a plant, animal, or person, adversity prompts the will to overcome through evolution and elevation. Hence the phrase "that which doesn't kill us, makes us stronger." If we have the emotional strength to live, if we understand our why, our purpose, we will not only live, we will prompt the transformation necessary to thrive.

We are privileged or granted divine cosmic knowledge only after we have endured enough resistance and suffering to expand our will to reach for the heavens.

Emotional Blueprint

Light represents the blueprint for human life and consciousness.

We grow from our fears and angers, processing our emotions in cycles that we hope will eventually mirror the wonders and divinity of the sun itself. The more fear and anger we learn to understand and integrate, the more joy and love we will have to share with the world.

The people who are actively digging into the shadows of themselves, who are trying to uncover the mystery of their blocks, the emotions of doubt which hold them back and prevent them from moving forward—the people who are able to process the emotions which have the potential to drain their energy, are the people who achieve greatness.

The people who let fear and doubt hold them back, the people who are unable to confront and process their feelings, allow their emotions to drain their life force and potential like a black hole.

The more we are able to accept, understand, integrate and elevate our emotions, the more we move from consuming life like a black hole, to radiating life like a star.

This is our dharma.

There is no bad, just counterpoints and complements which if integrated and processed properly, will expedite the process in our cycle of elevation, shifting our cycle from self-inflicted suffering, to achieving and harmonizing with our potential.

The Gravity of Love

Love is the force which holds or pulls everything together.

Love is close to acceptance and connection.

Love is many things, but the gateway to love is through acknowledgment. More so, the acknowledgement of something as it is, free of expectation, judgement or analysis. Acceptance is love.

The gravity of human love is powerful. In a sense, it is one of the most powerful forces in the universe. This is because human love not only transcends space and time, but attracts and persuades what we want or desire to us.

This is where emotional maturity and healthy boundaries come into play yet again. When we want something, instead of using love, the natural force of gravity to attract what we desire, we manipulate strands. We pull on strings, cords of joy which connect us to what we want. To our ears, these cords play sweet and enchanting music. Alas, but we are never satisfied with the tunes, for the true love which we desire is neglected. As we play with the strings of joy, cords which eventually produce notes and melodies of empty instant gratification, we venture further from love and lose our ability to find joy in all things.

Strings of Joy

Of the countless cords and strands that weave through us, connecting us to everything, our ambition can narrow our focus and energy to just the particular strands which we believe will fulfill our desires. Devoting the bulk of our emotional energy only to specific strands can cause us to neglect the countless other cords which are vital in supplying us with the information and energy of the universe itself. Disregarding the untold other cords which weave through us can also throw our emotional blueprint off balance. If we fall too far out of alignment with the cycle of elevation, we will stunt our growth and the ability to center ourselves in joy.

Joy is not only the light of our souls, it is the source of our energy. Reducing or restricting our energy can create or form a block in our cycle of elevation. This block can separate us from the source of energy which lights our soul. When this happens, a variety of emotional, mental, and physical illnesses can manifest.

Manipulation of Love

The gravity of love can also influence our ability to center ourselves in joy and block our cycle of elevation in another way.

Influence is a big word—the key word.

Love, or gravity, holds a radius of influence. This radius of influence pulls or attracts what is beneficial to us, what complements or is necessary to balance us, as well as what we desire and of course, what desires us. Emotional intelligence and healthy boundaries are essential in regulating the proper proportions of influence which we allow to pull or persuade our emotional blueprint. Emotional intelligence and healthy boundaries are also necessary to help us govern our own ambitions, what we pull toward our emotional blueprint.

Everything wants something and is desired by something. A flower for example, benefits from sun and rain. Light and water are necessary to balance the flower. Too much sun and not enough rain can harm the flower; too much water and not enough light can also harm the flower. Water and light are vital to the flower, but only in the proper proportions.

Water and light are beneficial to the health of the flower but the flower needs more. The flower's true desire is to proliferate and procreate. For the flower to achieve this goal and fulfill its desire, the flower employs charm and beauty. A flower can come in all different shapes, colors, and petal arrangements to help pull or attract what it desires, what it needs to help it proliferate: birds and bees.

Birds and bees hold their own radius of influence, but one of their desires is the flower. The desire of the birds and bees pull on and persuade the emotional blueprint of the flower. The flower responds to this pull and persuasion by generating and creating the colors and characteristics which will satisfy the desire of the birds and bees.

The flower holds a symbiotic relationship with the birds and bees. The flower needs messengers to carry its pollen to other flowers while the birds and bees need the flower to produce food. The color of the flower helps the birds and bees locate suitable sustenance. In this situation, everyone benefits while staying in alignment with the cycle of elevation.

The love between the flower and the birds and bees is free of emotional blocks. Balance and harmony are not only maintained, but created. The gravity of human love on the other hand, can be much trickier.

Human love can tend to fall out of alignment and not be so symbiotic. In many cases, human relationships can be convoluted and/or parasitic. This is because our desires and ambitions can break away from the complementary relationships which sustain balance and harmony. We have the freedom to detach or connect with whatever we wish. We can destroy or manipulate relationships to build and create whatever we desire.

Discord is one of the many ways we pay the price for true freedom, though the currency doesn't need to be so dramatic. We choose the form of payment to settle our debt for freedom; most just choose some form of suffering to zero out their balance.

The most valuable form of currency to pay our debt for freedom is service. This is because the true complement to freedom is service—in serving one another we all become free.

Desires and ambitions have their own radius of influence. For example, the flower desires the bee. For the flower to entice the bee, the flower's emotional blueprint must expand to encompass the bee's emotional blueprint. The flower extends her influence to overlap with the bee so she can establish a relationship. Once the flower understands the bee's emotional blueprint, then the flower persuades the bee to it through her very design. The flower decorates herself with the colors, scents and petal arrangements which the bee will find irresistible. The bee becomes emotionally and instinctually drawn to the flower. Through the bee's own emotional blueprint, the bee comes to desire the flower.

The flower and the bee unite by an undeniable force of nature.

Gravity.

The flower and the bee cultivate a relationship in service to one another, a relationship which ultimately sets them free.

Love.

Desires and ambitions produce a radius of influence which set the tone for the type of relationship between partners. In the case of the flower and the bee, it is a symbiotic relationship. In the case of humans and almost everything we desire, there is a huge emphasis on parasitic relationships.

In a parasitic relationship, our desires and ambitions can persuade our emotional blueprint to redesign itself, to betray its authenticity, just to attract some artificial external coordinate with no foundation in any sort of harmonious or symbiotic relationship. Instead of mutual benefit through the proper proportions of complements (so harmony can be created and maintained), a parasitic relationship is established, which damages and destroys the union of the parties involved for the sole benefit of one. Parasitic relationships pull us farther away from true love and joy.

With the freedom we are gifted, humans tend to establish parasitic relationships through the manipulation and perversion of love, and thus, are pulled ever further from true love and joy.

When we seek to alter what is, to manipulate something to what we want it to be for our own personal gain, without regard or respect for balance (the source of energy which breathes life into everything), we fall out of alignment with the cycle of elevation. When we become blocked from the cycle of elevation, from the source of energy which sustains all of existence, we reject the true nourishment it provides in favor of artificial sustenance. We become parasites, syphoning artificial energy from the coordinates we seek to attain. In turn, this imitation energy persuades our emotional blueprint to alter its authentic form into something which can process this synthetic energy into something which can preserve our existence.

Many relationships we engage in are like this, especially romantic ones. Romantic relationships often consist of fabricated realities and selfish desires which are projected onto one another. These romantic relationships divert all participating parties off the path of true love and joy to pursue cords and strands which lead away from it. We follow these strings to some counterfeit, manufactured fantasy of love which is both inauthentic and unsustainable.

This fake love provides artificial energy which we feed on like parasites. Unfortunately, this bogus energy we consume is unable to sustain our life force or to help us grow into our potential. We are left feeling empty and lost.

Without the emotional intelligence to understand our illusion saturated endeavors toward love, without the healthy boundaries which keep us aligned and in balance with the cycle of elevation, we gravitate toward oblivion.

The Law of Attraction

Why do opposites (or complements) attract?

Deep down there is a part of us which wants to unite with the things we essentially don't understand, we yearn for what we are not, and we desire what we lack.

Without emotional intelligence and healthy boundaries, we are subject to self-inflicted misery and emotional trauma because we cannot properly balance the complementary forces which we seek to integrate. Instead of elevation, we end up getting sucked deeper into a black hole of emotional discord.

It's not about choosing what's right, or the light, or what makes you feel good which will eventually lead you to joy and happiness. It's about learning how to integrate the things in life which you associate with fear and anger, so you may process the energies which are stunting your growth and holding you back.

When we transform negative energy into knowledge and understanding, we can expand or amplify our ability to experience, embody, and radiate joy and love.

Many people run from their problems, hide or mask what is bothering them, or even project their fears and angers toward something or someone else. Emotional accountability requires us to take responsibility and ownership for our feelings; feelings that are hard to accept as a part of who we are. We can associate these feelings with weakness or vulnerability, pushing away or trying to eradicate what doesn't feel right or good to us. What most don't realize is that vulnerability opens up a path to true strength.

Vulnerability, if nurtured and cultivated properly, leads us to our greatest power and potential, for vulnerability calls forth courage—the courage to be seen when the world seems to want to keep us small and hidden. It is through vulnerability that we can begin to accept the aspects of ourselves which we are ashamed of. When we acknowledge the whole of who we are, we needn't fear being seen or found anymore, for we accept who and what we are with dignity and grace.

If we give in to vulnerability and hide, then we choose a cowardly path where each step leaves a footprint of regret. If we reject the feelings and emotions which don't align with who we want to be, or how we view ourselves, then we regret who and what we are while denying a very real part of ourselves. We inhibit the relationship which will form a bridge from the unknown to the known—a bridge of courage which will help reveal our true nature and an authentic understanding of our potential.

We must understand our true self before we can begin to uncover our true potential.

Without a star there is no black hole, and without a black hole there is no star.

Life and death are the same way, so are love and fear, joy and anger.

We cannot live only on one side or in only one aspect. If we try to purify ourselves (or the world) through the eradication of a complement (good or evil, life or death, love or hate) by projecting our beliefs onto others, then we can create the illusion of separate states and opposite perspectives.

A selfish pursuit of love or God can eventually turn into a lust which systematically removes all aspects of love or God from our lives. The manipulation of love or god through our own self-centered desires can remove the essence of love or God which we wish to connect with. Our original desire for a relationship with love or god can become perverted and ultimately severed from the source of its divinity. It can almost be said that the pursuit of purity leads to corruption and cleaves that which we wish to connect with from its true meaning and purpose.

The purpose of life isn't to change anyone. The reality is we can't change anyone, we can only expand perspectives through authentic relationships. Our minds are very protective of the belief structures we have created, because our belief structures guard our emotions. To gain access to the mind, we must first appeal to the heart. Emotions will open the mind to new perspectives and a broader definition of love only when an emotional connection is established. This emotional connection motivates the mind to accept, understand, and integrate new experiences and feelings which were once perceived as threats.

If the purpose of life isn't to change people, or to change the world, then what is it? This is a question you must answer for yourself, but for me, the purpose of life is to expand my own emotional blueprint so I may experience a broader definition of love and God.

As I establish the kind of authentic connections and relationships which expand my emotional blueprint, the more I understand that it's not my job to change anyone. My job is to stand next to the people and creatures which I have cultivated a relationship with. From loving and healthy relationships, we can develop in the ways we were meant to, not as others would intend us to. I must not be offended when I come across someone who wishes to not accept and integrate my beliefs as part of their perspectives. We must all respect the limitations and boundaries of each other. A person may not be ready to incorporate the core beliefs you may embody, and in truth, he/or she may never be ready, but this should not prevent the establishment of a respectful and working relationship. Every perspective is valid, even if they never merge or unite with yours.

When we march our morals and values to the doorstep of others through force, then the good we wish to spread is received as evil. When we deny ourselves the connection and completion of a circuit because we believe something to be separate or opposite from us, then we can unintentionally disrupt the relationships of energy, the harmonious and symbiotic relationships which connect everything as part of a collective multidimensional web of cycles made possible by light and gravity: joy and love.

May light and love guide you on your journey.

Crystallization

When we try and manipulate energy, we can interrupt and even stop the flow—the natural cycle of energy. When we become too overwhelmed or scared, or are just too set in our beliefs to adapt, evolve, and integrate the changing of times with respect to the cycles, then we can create a block. We get stuck in a stasis which prevents progress and growth. We may find a way to live in this sterile state, but we surely don't feel alive and we are definitely not living, just surviving.

Being too rigid in our ways, keeping our boundaries too tight and crystallizing our doctrines in a fortification of faith creates a monotonous, artificial cycle which removes us from the natural flow, the natural cycle of elevation. Again, we may be alive, but we are not living because we are not connected to the life force, the flow of limitless potential and energy which feeds and hydrates the soul.

Artificial Energy

When we are not connected we require more energy to sustain the artificial life we have created.

Our artificial life includes living in the world which humans have manufactured—our cities, roads, governments and institutions— everything we've built so we don't have to interact with the forces of nature. This artificial world we've created for ourselves and volunteered to live in is harder to navigate than the natural world which surrounds us because in our artificial world, we hide facts, deny truth and chase illusion.

We hide facts, deny truth, and chase illusion by seeking to understand something not as it is but as we would make it or want it to be. We would often rather live in a world defined by artificial parameters in order to instill our own incomplete or manipulated definition onto whatever it is that we desire. We want the world to be how we would want it to be—the way which makes it the most comfortable for us—within our understanding or lack of understanding.

In contrast, real relationships require work. The foundation of these authentic relationships is built on mutual benefit and respect. We often don't want to put in the work to cultivate authentic relationships. Instead, we wish for everything to respect us without having to respect anything in return. We wish to conquer and control.

We must develop an authentic relationship with ourselves if we wish to cultivate any real understanding of the world. If we connect to the reasons behind our desires and actions then we can reveal our why, our purpose. The ultimate purpose for anything in existence is to connect with its complement. The union of complements in service to one another form symbiotic relationships. These harmonious connections perpetuate an exchange of energy which expands life with respect to all of existence.

When we are not connected, we require artificial energy.

Some people think that money is the root of all evil, while others say the root of all evil is the lack of money. What we forget is that money is just a concept, a tool—a tool that way too many people rely on, yet know very little about. Most people know as much about money as they do about themselves, which isn't much to say the least.

Since we don't know what is real, most of us spend our energy like many of us spend our money: foolishly and recklessly. If we knew what our energy represented and how valuable it is (like money) we would not be so careless and foolhardy with how we spend it. Our external actions and aspirations mirror our internal efforts and pursuits.

As vampires are dependent upon sucking the blood of another to sustain life, we often rely on draining the energy and resources around us to survive in our fabricated world.

It's not money or the lack of money, which causes suffering (though poverty is a factor), it is the lack of connection to the flow, an absence of a sincere and authentic relationship with ourselves and, I'll say it again, but the word may be imbued with a different meaning altogether for you than for me—God. It is our connection to our emotions, our relationship with divinity and nature, which illuminates the soul.

Harmonious emotional connections and symbiotic relationships define a joyful existence with respect to every experience love can offer.

Energy Work

Learn about yourself, understand yourself, and develop yourself truly and authentically.

This means work and effort—lots of it.

To manage the many so-called "mistakes" which you will make, you will need to cultivate emotional endurance and fortitude.

Mistakes are necessary to serve as lessons. Each mistake represents a part of you which you are pulling out of the shadows, a part of you that you must integrate and unite with in order to reveal your true potential and power.

Once you see the whole truth, the big picture, integrating your mistakes and acquiring what you desire will be attained much easier. For example, you may desire more money, which is essentially stored energy. The stored energy money represents is exchanged for time. Time like money, if spent wisely, can be used to cultivate healthy relationships which blossom into the resources necessary to provide options. Options—viable, lucrative, productive options—and plenty of them, are what makes one wealthy and desirable to others.

Being desirable keeps you in demand and increases your gravitational pull and radius of influence. This is the law of attraction.

Abundance draws wealth.

The larger and denser a thing is, like planets and stars in space, the greater their gravitational pull and radius of influence. An abundance of money and a wealth of time (the acquisition of energy and power is like the accumulation of matter which forms a dense star or planet) expands one's gravitational pull and radius of influence, making it easier to develop harmonious emotional connections and symbiotic relationships. As time is increased and stress is reduced, the law of attraction begins to favor you more and more as you begin to draw in the health, wealth and relationships required to provide you with the options necessary to manage your life with ease.

Seeing the big picture allows the path of abundance and wealth to

101

reveal itself and promotes an emotional drive to get there, thus reducing the impression of obstacles along the way.

No matter how effortlessly money flows your way, you must always respect it.

Go about any endeavor in this fashion, not just the pursuit of money, and align yourself more and more with the flow of energy cycling all around you, and you will cease to be a vampire, or worse, an emotionless zombie who wanders through life with no purpose.

Pursue purpose with respect to time, money, and waste so you may feel alive again. Connect to the meaning and purpose behind your existence.

Make your inner child proud of who you have become and are becoming.

Walk with the vivid, vibrant vitality you once embodied as a young person discovering the wonders of your potential and the magic of the world around you.

Vibrations

Energy (emotion) translates into vibration.

Lower vibrations are associated with feelings of sadness, anger and fear. Stress encompasses so many emotions which are associated with low vibrations that the body begins to deteriorate and degenerate.

Love, happiness, and joy are associated with high vibrations. If you want to operate at a higher frequency, if you want to be in the upper level of the vibrational spectrum, then embody positivity.

Emotions are literally the gateway to achieving longevity, health, and overall success in life. Magic (energy, aka money) is attracted to high frequency vibrations like a magnet. Emotions of wellbeing—joy and love—are the most effective ways to achieve success in anything. Joy and love are also the most effective means to connect with anyone, including yourself.

The Masculine and the Feminine

As far as energy is concerned, there are two aspects which humans have come to intimately understand. These two concepts of energy have endured the rise and fall of many civilizations and dynasties. These two concepts are the masculine and the feminine energies.

The Earth is wrapped in feminine energy (formation), represented by Mother Nature.

Mother Nature is the goddess of creation. The existence of everything in the universe was, is, and always will be conceived through feminine energy.

Existence in and of itself is a miracle, but to only just exist is the definition of loneliness.

To quell the loneliness, all of creation, all of existence is woven together and connected by an ever-moving and ever-cycling, inter-and-multi-dimensional web, held together by the gravity of love.

Connection through this web may quell the protest of loneliness, but it is still not enough. All of creation, all that exists, still yearns for more. That more is satisfied through the experience of relationships, authentic connections which begin from within us and extend outward to all that surrounds us.

This is why emotion is at the root of all existence. Through emotion, through feeling, we can experience the connection, the bond we share with everything.

Just as there is a force behind a star (a black hole) which transforms fear and anger into joy and love, radiating as light and gravity from the sun, Mother Nature requires a force, an energy to help her manifest potential into reality.

That force is masculine energy.

If the Earth is enveloped in feminine energy, then the sun radiates masculine energy (potential).

Mother Nature transforms the light, the masculine energy it receives from the sun into the formation of life itself. Everything is manifested from light (masculine energy) and converted into existence through Mother Nature (feminine energy).

Masculine energy seeks out feminine energy so he can transition from potential into reality, and feminine energy seeks out masculine energy to create life in one form of existence or another, so she can share the experience of connection to all.

The Lonely Paradox

Masculine energy by itself is lonely potential.

Feminine energy by itself is lonely existence.

Masculine energy is accustomed to enduring long periods of lonely potential, the possibility of being or becoming while searching and waiting to be embraced by Mother Nature (feminine energy) so he can come into existence.

Masculine energy seeks to unite with feminine energy so he can manifest and be born into a form which can experience the life and connection he so desires and longs for.

Anything that comes into existence wishes first to experience the energy which brought it to life. The first connection that anything seeks when born is its creator. We gravitate toward what we came from.

Our biological mother represents more than just our physical creator, but a connection to the feminine energy of Mother Nature, the goddess of creation herself. Thus, we are always compelled to stay connected and remain bonded with her in one way or another. This is why all the wild places—the rivers, the trees, and the mountains—call to us.

Existence itself experiences life through Mother Nature, through the connection feminine energy provides.

While the potential for life, for existence itself, resides in the light of masculine energy, he cannot come into form without his complement—feminine energy.

Masculine energy desires feminine energy, and feminine energy desires masculine energy. Another beautiful example of a symbiotic relationship in service to one another. In various proportions, the masculine and feminine come together as complements. It is all detailed in the many declarations of the gravity of love.

The Moods of Men

Masculine energy cannot experience anything without feminine energy. Without feminine energy, masculine energy remains lost in a sea of potential. A lack of feminine energy is why many men seem to get stuck in moods.

If a man is disconnected from feminine energy for too long, he can revert into the state of his archetype: potential energy. This is usually when men are unable to motivate themselves to accomplish something or finish projects they started.

Masculine energy endures a form of loneliness which represents the archetype of its aspect: a sort of lonely indifference.

If a man is unable to connect with an external form of feminine energy, or the feminine aspect within himself (i.e., "the anima"), then he can become very singular in his pursuits, and thus, disconnected, hard, stern, and stoic toward his environment.

When the masculine and feminine energies are able to form a symbiotic relationship with one another and dance in harmony, when they unite as one, the masculine and feminine energies experience a form of elevated union. This divine bond establishes a connection with all of existence.

The value of this merger is many times greater than the sum of energies which came together to create it. What is birthed from this commixture is a vision of exquisite beauty—the elevation of our potential.

This is how life, reality and existence are elevated. This is the progression of consciousness.

The Yin and the Yang of Quantum Mechanics

Everything in existence, all of creation, is not of a single aspect, a solitary energy of either feminine or masculine, but a combination of both in some variant.

The essence or archetype of feminine and masculine energy exists in the spaces between worlds.

These spaces are inhabited by measurements and math—dynamic algorithms which flow and fluctuate. Numbers which seem to appear and vanish all at once. This is the space where quantum mechanics rule. Where quantum objects can operate in more than one form, like in particles and waves.

This is where distance is both meaningful and irrelevant at the same time due to something humans have dubbed "quantum entanglement." Where a change in one area of space will instantly create a change in another area, no matter the distance.

Another phenomenon which takes place in space (quantum mechanics takes place everywhere, not just space, but space is a good place to imagine all of this) is the ability for something to be in two places at the same time: quantum superposition.

How is all this possible?

Math and physics are highly specialized disciplines which focus on narrow aspects in what is actually quite a large field of study: the proof of existence and reality.

Math and physics are able to grasp and explain only so much because these areas of study are incomplete without the knowledge and understanding of their complements.

When it comes to the existence and reality of the universe, the scope and study of knowledge must span the distance from what is known to what is unknown. We must extend our reach from what we believe will give us definite and finite answers, to what will defy and disprove everything we ever conceived or thought possible about existence and reality.

Emotion is the complement to math.

Emotion is what math responds to.

Emotion is why math, in quantum mechanics, doesn't respond the way we want it to.

In quantum mechanics we are unable to predict the outcome. This is because within the field of quantum mechanics, emotion is influencing the sequence, the very structure of math itself.

There are countless algorithms, equations and areas of study within the field of math which have yet to be discovered.

We are unable to obtain finite answers or forecast solid conclusions because emotion defies all logic.

Emotions cause a ripple effect which persuade and arouse countless other emotional ripple effects to activate. This chain of "cause and effect" prompts the entire web of existence to respond accordingly—not in a predictable, domino effect sort of way, but in a highly emotional, and thus, highly unpredictable way.

The ripple effect is unpredictable because there are endless variants and values to account for which are constantly changing due to dynamic emotional factors.

Time and space don't form a straight line, but are multi-dimensional concepts (which bloom more like a flower) to form a platform of infinite possibilities. Even the chain of effect isn't represented traditionally. Each link in the so called "chain" is actually a cycle. Each cycle is linked to countless other cycles which are linked with countless other cycles and so on and so forth, forming a multi-dimensional "blossom" of existence.

All forms in the universe, including the space between forms (dark matter) are composed of an emotional blueprint housed in a structure of math to carry and convey these ripples (or messages) to the far reaches of the galaxy.

I'm sure this is all confusing, but if that is not enough of an explanation, especially when one contemplates the tremendous distance between planets and solar systems and galaxies, what, if any answer should be sufficient to justify so much "empty space"?

Why would any math or emotion be needed to fill this so called "void" between heavenly bodies?

To answer this question, we have to recognize and appreciate the prospect that there is still so much potential we have yet to discover and manifest just within ourselves, let alone the universe. Then we have to wonder how much of that "empty space" or potential is required to expand and elevate not just ourselves, but all forms of creation. If there are countless creations, all of which hold the possibility of infinite potential to expand and evolve, then we need all this "blank space" just so all of creation has a fair chance and opportunity to elevate.

A great example of evolution and elevation requiring space to expand is found in the very design of our dwellings. We have come so far from the modest shelters we once called home. From humble huts to extraordinary skyscrapers, the architecture of our emotional blueprint continues to expand, evolve, and elevate toward the heavens, extending into the endless vacuum of space.

Even in the profound abyss of space, our potential and purpose bleeds into every blank corner to occupy every hollow cavity of the seemingly endless spaces between worlds. It is here, in the areas which seem to be void of life, where we experience a renaissance of design (math) and inspiration (emotion) which greet our cognizance with miraculous possibility. We harness this quantum potential to erect monuments which serve as a testament to the advancement of our civilization and divine consciousness as a species.

When we expand our consciousness, we venture into the deep and seemingly empty realms of outer space. It is in these nether regions of space which we believe to be null of existence, that we discover and experience highly elevated and advanced structures (math) and emotions (joy and love) which arouse our soul (emotional blueprint) to pursue and embrace enlightenment.

What the nether regions reveal is unique to the questions of the individual. What we discover is a distinct experience relative to our emotional blueprint. These distinct experiences unveil unique revelations about our meaning and purpose this time around, and are yet another example of how and why all emotion or versions of reality are valid.

When an emotion changes in me, it influences the whole chemical structure I am made of. It is almost as if I have no choice and that free will and the autonomy to make my own decisions are false concepts (but you can make decisions and you do have free will, for we have been granted the divine gift of choice).

Think of a time when you felt completely satisfied, then you came upon something, or something came upon you, which shifted your mood to an extreme. Whether you transitioned to happy, sad, angry, afraid... etc., your whole biological structure also shifted instantly. You were ready to mourn, to fight, to flee, to jump for joy.

The mood of an entire stadium of people can shift instantaneously during the final moments of a sports game, especially if the scores are tied.

The energy of a get-together can change dramatically and even all at once if a person who was uninvited and not generally accepted shows up.

The vibe at a concert can instantly swing in one direction or another in relation to the song the band chooses to play.

Emotion operates in all aspects, encompassing the extremes of all spectrums; it is here and there at the same time, operating in all forms possible at once. More so, emotion is undefinable and unburdened or unconfined; it is free from things like time and distance.

Emotion is what gives quantum mechanics dimension.

Emotion [love and joy (gravity and light)] is woven into every possible algorithm.

When presented with a choice, emotion takes all choices.

You cannot simultaneously know two properties of a quantum object (any emotion) because in doing so, you would prove emotion as finite, as real, as it is of objective existence. We may experience an objective existence, but existence itself is subjective.

This is an over-simplified and very rough explanation. Think of quantum properties as coordinates of longitude and latitude on a plane or graph. Coordinates of longitude and latitude are usually represented with X as the horizontal axis and Y as the vertical axis. For this example, let's substitute X and Y with—time and place. Outside of quantum mechanics, you can trace an event or transaction by knowing these two properties.

When you have finite parameters which are applicable outside of quantum mechanics like time and place, you can navigate your environment fairly easily. When we do this, we are basically saying that our world is finite and fallible. We are saying that we can predict what is going to happen, and more-so, make something happen through the influence of our desires in relation to the data provided.

We study what happened so we may understand what is currently happening so we can predict what is going to happen. With finite parameters, we can come to understand what a particular point in space did, is doing, or will look like with two very basic properties like—time and place. The desired outcomes and predictability which finite parameters provide falls apart in quantum mechanics.

In the realm of quantum mechanics, you can never simultaneously know two quantum properties. In quantum mechanics if you know the time, you will never know the place. If you know the place, you will never know the time.

For quantum mechanics (math and emotion) to produce infinite possibilities while simultaneously sustaining our existence, our concept of rules and laws must expand.

If a time is known, the place cannot be bound to a specific area. It would dispel quantum mechanics altogether. Rather, knowing a quantum property such as "time" would give way to the infinite possibilities of quantum mechanics (math and emotion) and generate the answer for the second quantum element in question "place" as everywhere, or all places, with the possibility of nowhere, or not even existing at all. The same applies if the quantum property which represented "place" was known. The coordinate for "time" would be all possible times, or all the time, with the possibility of no-time, or not occurring ever.

Measurable locations occurring at specific times would prove quantum mechanics as fallible, because in theory, we would figure out a way to disprove or improve upon it.

Math by its very nature is infallible.

Emotion is infallible because it is subjective. Emotion can be anything, experienced at any time, to any extent and to all extremes.

Emotion takes all possible paths because it is all possible paths. Every emotion that can be experienced is experienced. Everything that can happen does happen. This is because emotion isn't something that you can predict or measure. You can neither prove that it exists nor that it doesn't exist.

Emotion is a subjective experience which produces infinite possibilities, perspectives and versions of reality.

Emotion attracts and persuades the quantum structures of math to assemble in devout service to the unconditional love of all creation. You have to remember that everything, from the cosmos to all of nature, inanimate or animate, has a desire, and in turn, is also desired.

The cumulative desire of all of existence prompts the cycle of elevation and generates the unlimited potential of the universe. This is the way the universe conspires to give everything, all of creation, what it feels or believes it desires in one way or another. So, be careful what you wish for, you just might get it.

The void of space is saturated with the essence of potential energy and formation energy.

Like zeros and ones in computer programming, these energies produce and create the spectrum of existence.

This is where the possibility of something and the possibility of nothing create the most extravagant, awesome and impossible phenomena.

The Predicament of Living Extreme

If we dwell too deeply within the masculine aspect, then we may become lost in a lonely sea of potential energy, floating in an ocean of possibilities.

If one embraces the energy or aspect of potential and possibility, he or she may be able to receive messages of insight and inspiration—however, without the connection to the feminine aspect, he or she will not be able to transform their potential into reality.

On the other hand, if one lives too far within the feminine aspect, immersed too deeply in the material world, then he or she will experience a heightened sensitivity to their surroundings. Existence will be an overwhelming sea of emotion, for the feminine aspect, the feminine archetype, wishes just to share the beauty and experience of creation and connection through emotion.

To balance living in the extreme nature of the feminine aspect, one must embrace masculine energy by engaging in activities of potential and possibility. This is anything creative, because to be creative is to harness the potential of what can be.

The CREATION of something through potential is the transition from masculine energy to feminine energy. The *concept* of playing, stories, music, art, etc. are masculine, while the actual manifestation of said themes into composition is feminine. This is why some people love to bake, cook, grow gardens, go for walks and create connections. Creativity doesn't need to be fancy to remove blocks. Small acts of consistent creativity help to move stagnant or stuck energy along so our emotions can harmonize with the grand cycle of existence.

Potential Reality

Initiating and engaging the masculine energy of possibility without seeing it through to completion can block our emotional cycle and make us feel stuck in a space of lonely potential. Without expressing and executing the inspiration provided to us by emotion, our genius creativity would be wasted and the brilliant ideas bestowed upon us by revelation would remain trapped in the sea of possibility.

Being stuck or lost in the space of potential can shift us out of alignment, blocking our ability to flow and severing the connection we have to ourselves, our cycle, and our relationship with joy and love.

Lost in an ocean of potential, we become uncertain of who we are and how to proceed with our lives. We may even become unsure with the concept of existence itself.

Though we have the free will and capacity to do anything, without the connection to the feminine energy which would propel us into action so that we may manifest our potential into reality, we become dormant, lost in the space of potential reality.

Chapter 7

The Way of the Warrior

Chapter seven continues to break down common concepts and characteristics which seem to generate conflict within people.

A warrior uses his environment to his advantage, while a victim struggles with his environment. A victim blames his environment for his suffering, while a warrior adapts to his environment so he may thrive.

A true warrior balances the complements of good and evil within him. Through practice and discipline, a warrior learns to accept the complementary energies which swirl in every corner of existence.

Our potential flowers into purpose by merging the light and shadow of who we are.

A victim denies the complementary energies within himself, restraining his true nature. The suppression of one's true nature is expressed through neurotic behaviors which breed illness and emotional discord. One of the most prominent symptoms of a victim is the projection of external blame.

A warrior is in harmony with the energies of good and evil and all the complementary energies which compose his emotional blueprint, his true nature. A warrior embraces the creative creation of all complementary energies, energies which are responsible for the infinite possibilities of existence itself.

Martial Arts

I have always loved martial arts.

I love the way a master martial artist can either out-position his opponent or move and manipulate his opponent's position to his own advantage with flawless physical technique and controlled emotions.

When I was younger, I took a few Jiu-jitsu classes. The whole thing for me was pretty intimidating due to how close and intimate I needed to be with total strangers.

The intimidation factor grew even greater because I was completely new to the martial-art and everyone else looked way more comfortable and thus, way more dangerous than me—that was my perspective anyway. Being new, I felt like I had little to no chance at harming anyone.

It wasn't just because I was new that I felt this way. I didn't like conflict and had never even theorized about getting into a fight. I basically viewed myself as a harmless individual and thus, a relatively good person.

I believe that this benign-and-thus-good self-image is one way the timid can view or relate to themselves. What I came to understand about the idea of "if I can do no harm," or better yet, "if I am incapable of doing any harm, then I am a good person" is that it is just plain rubbish.

Gandhi-Jitsu

It is not well known, but Gandhi himself praised Japanese soldiers who wielded the martial art of jiu-jitsu against Russian soldiers in the Russo-Japanese war.

Though Gandhi's philosophy consisted of a strict nonviolence policy, it was said that he used political Jiu-Jitsu to persuade the movements of his opponent (British Colonialism) to expose their own weakness (violent repression) to the world. Some of his nonviolent tactics included nonviolent protest and the peaceful disobeying of authorities, thus inspiring peaceful mass mobilizations of non-compliance, and initiating boycotts of goods and services.

Though Gandhi was a pacifist, he understood the art of war.

Gandhi perhaps embodied the art of nonviolence, yet he still adopted a martial method to stop the bullying (the submission and slavery) of his people. Gandhi acted and took control of the situation (violent repression) by strategizing with the grace of a master martial artist, to coerce the movements of his opponent and out-maneuver the British Empire.

Bad Victim

The point is, if you are being targeted as a victim, you shouldn't just let yourself be taken advantage of and do nothing. You can't adopt the harmless victim mentality and expect to be viewed as an exceptional and/or good human being. You need to expose your value and your right to live by unleashing your will to survive.

If you believe in nonviolence as Gandhi did then great, but you still have to act in the face of adversity.

Don't cry out as a helpless-to-violence do-gooder person waiting for someone like Gandhi to save you. An ignorant bully will always mistake your kindness for weakness.

Even as a devout pacifist, Gandhi held great authority and was respected.

I'm not telling you to physically fight back or get revenge on someone who wronged you. I am hoping instead that you will shift perspectives so you can educate yourself on how you may handle situations, especially conflict, in a more effective way. When I say effective, I mean the most beneficial and peaceful way to resolve a situation for everyone involved as possible.

Diplomacy

What we have to remember with all this talk about cultivating a unique emotional blueprint, is that just because you believe you shine the brightest when you behave a certain way, doesn't give you the right to be obnoxious about it. Gandhi didn't go around shoving his beliefs in people's faces like, "Hey, look at me, I'm Gandhi, and I am better than you because I figured out a way to start a revolution and halt the oppression of my people without violence. You should all praise and worship me, for I am more enlightened than most of you will ever be."

Gandhi was diplomatic and graceful with his beliefs. Gandhi did what he could in a way which did not compromise who he was. His selfless acts benefited his people and the world as he stayed true to himself. Gandhi didn't believe that preaching his philosophy would change the circumstances of his people and the world. Instead, Gandhi embodied his beliefs and acted whenever the right opportunity presented itself to demonstrate his philosophy in a way his words never could.

When we discover our emotional blueprint and embark on our personal journey toward our potential, we should definitely celebrate, but we do not have the right to shove it in the faces of other people. Just because we are finally comfortable in our own skin doesn't justify making other people feel uncomfortable by being annoying about it. We still need social skills. We still need to practice social etiquette… to a certain degree. For there are times when diplomacy may even go too far.

When we are forced to conform, in an uncomfortable way, or in a way in which we sacrifice our own dignity in the name of diplomacy, then it begins to be more about silent oppression and less about diplomacy. The line between diplomacy and oppression is a little different for everyone. Only you can determine where your limits and boundaries are, and only you can manage how much you are willing to tolerate when this line is crossed.

Know who you are, celebrate who you are, share your gifts with the world, but be as diplomatic as possible about it. You will find many people who celebrate with you and embrace your true self, but you will also come across many people who are not yet ready to accept who you are and what you stand for. You do not need to shove your philosophy in the faces of these people or to be offensive about it, nor should these people demand you to be silent by oppressing you.

The line between diplomacy and oppression will be crossed many times. As you cultivate your response to these trespasses, your true self will be revealed more and more. As your authentic self emerges, you may find you are less affected by so many trivial offences as you bathe in joy. You have to find your harmony, your own diplomacy within the world. Your diplomacy may even turn into the simple act of spreading joy.

Do-Gooder Victim

Now back to the story of my initial Jiu-Jitsu classes.

In all honesty I didn't really care about learning Jiu-Jitsu, I really just enjoyed watching and admiring the fancy, graceful movements between people from a distance. I didn't really care to be the one grappling and fighting.

During this stage in my life, I was more like a do-gooder person who believed that because I was sensitive and incapable of doing harm, that I was essentially good, and thus, no harm would come to me.

Boy was I wrong! One of the first times that lesson was revealed to me with complete transparency was during those Jiu-Jitsu classes.

Beneath the Boot

I thought that if I could convey how harmless and innocent I was to my sparring partner, he or she would have mercy on me and not grind me onto the mat like an ant under a boot. That was my plan anyway and I stuck to it.

Not only was I squished like a bug, I was bent into positions which just felt wrong in every way. I was folded into shapes like a giant piece of origami paper, into configurations which didn't even seem possible.

I mean, who would fold paper to look like a person who was trying to go to the bathroom but then got stuck in the toilet bowl with the seat around an arm and the lid smashing against their head? I don't even know how to fold that with paper, let alone with an actual living person.

Brown Stripe

The projection of my harmless self to invoke mercy was a complete and utter failure.

Most of the people who I sparred with had belts within the lower to middle end of the colored belt ranking system. Needless to say, they were all eager to test their abilities and practice what they had been learning on someone who they could bend into submission.

Then I spared with a brown belt.

I was completely terrified. I knew a person who sported a brown belt was just around the corner from achieving a black belt, a freaking master martial artist.

Just by the way the brown belt carried himself, I could tell he could do some serious damage and was more than capable of inflicting massive amounts of harm to me. I trembled at the thought of what this person could fold me into.

The Good Advantage

All this scary, anxious anticipation was for nothing.

The brown belt was patient and allowed me to try and move him in ways which would give me the advantage. After I failed, he would square us off again. He allowed me to try several strategies but displayed to me his superior positioning and the faults in my movements.

The brown belt would then show me the correct way to pin him by maneuvering me with flawless technique into a pin. He would then walk me through the steps to maneuver him into a position which was to my advantage.

It was at that moment that I understood what really defined a person as being "good."

Here was someone who wielded supreme knowledge and power over me, who could twist my limbs and pummel my body to the ground, yet he showed me much more than mercy, he showed me knowledge. He acknowledged my lower status and proceeded to lift me up to a higher level through his superior expertise.

The Good, the Bad, and the Balanced

Being "good" isn't the ability to impose your will onto others, nor is it being a harmless, helpless victim.

Being "good" is having the ability to do harm and choosing not to.

We can even raise the bar of "good" to a new level by saying that "good" is not only having the ability to do harm and choosing not to, but cultivating every possible route to resolve a situation, with harm being a last resort and only inflicted to the least extent necessary to settle a situation.

A person who is "good" knows how to cultivate and integrate his or her ability to do harm without succumbing to its destructive nature.

We need to tap into the shadowy places within ourselves, the aspects which we may not want to identify as part of who we are, like our ability to do harm or our destructive nature. These shadowy aspects are usually referred to as something unrefined, raw, and wild. We need to keep our wild nature alive and healthy to have an edge over the constant challenges in life.

We should not seek to eradicate what we don't like or don't understand.

Our wild nature grants us the ability to harness and wield our emotional power when confronted with opposition. Our wild edge keeps us alert and vigilant while also allowing us to adapt, evolve and flow with the sometimes harsh movements of life. When we are able to build a relationship with the aspects of ourselves that we wish to hide and suppress, we are able to unify and integrate our true power, understand our true ability, and reveal our true nature.

Someone who wields true power with a balanced perspective of his nature and his abilities, like the brown belt I sparred with, will not do harm unless absolutely necessary. Above that, he will seek to help others to discover and connect with the aspects hiding within themselves so they may also come into their true power, understand their true ability, and reveal their true nature.

Denial is a River within You

The shadowy aspects do not only include the ability to do harm or our destructive nature but also include any number of other aspects which we do not understand.

If we deny, suppress, or seek to eliminate the aspect(s) of ourselves which we are uncomfortable with (the shadowy aspects), then, in the best-case scenario, we are unbalanced or incomplete. What tends to happen, though, is that a person seeks to only live within the aspect in which he or she is comfortable.

Denying the relationship between the aspects of ourselves that we are comfortable with and the aspects of ourselves which we are uncomfortable with will eventually spill over into the way we build and maintain relationships in our lives.

Defining yourself—crystallizing yourself—within an aspect limits your potential within a certain belief structure. Having such well-defined parameters for existence ultimately creates conflict when trying to interact with anything and everything which falls outside the framework of your limited perspective.

The most successful professional cage fighters train in multiple disciplines and use the tool-sets of multiple martial arts in combat.

Critical Conflict

If we suppress our wild nature and deny a relationship with our true self, conflict begins to arise within us. This conflict can extend outward to external relationships.

Conflict isn't a bad thing, but too much, especially when the conflict creates a duality within ourselves, can give rise to neurotic behavior. If one is not willing to change, grow or compromise to build a healthy, symbiotic relationship, then the possibility of coming to an understanding, even of oneself, becomes impossible. To avoid and/or justify conflict, one becomes critical.

Being overly-critical to the point that it creates neuroticism is a defense mechanism used by people who chose to live sensitive, painful lives of self-imprisonment within the confines of their aspect. Since people feel safe within their structure, within the boundaries of their aspect, they become exceedingly neurotic about maintaining the safety of their stronghold. This is different from a teacher being critical of his or her student for the sake of that student's improvement. Everyone needs to be broken down a little bit so that they can build themselves up in a better way.

The neurotic person is exceedingly critical about the way others live and most importantly, the way that they live. Everything needs to be exact. Everything needs to be done by the rules which help define and maintain their world. They wish for the world to conform to them rather than to construct a healthy, symbiotic relationship with what and how the world actually is. Ultimately, this neuroticism causes them to become their own worst enemy, for they are most critical of themselves.

Neurotic by Nature

Neuroticism is a limiting factor when it comes to success. The critical nature of neurotic people, especially toward themselves, lowers their social status in the dominance hierarchy.

More often than not, neurotic people lower themselves on the dominance hierarchy even before a formal hierarchy has even been established. This creates a self-limiting ceiling which they are unable rise above, for a neurotic person will submit to anyone who has more confidence in the areas of life which they are unfamiliar with.

Authority and rules become their truth, rather than truth becoming their guiding authority.

The Blame Game

A neurotic person limits themselves within the confines of their environment. The neurotic person blames their environment or their circumstance as the reason for their lack of growth as well as their failure to succeed in whatever enterprise they are currently pursuing.

Emotional Illness

Being overly critical ultimately limits how one may experience reality. All of the limits which an overly-critical, neurotic person places on themselves ends up affecting their own emotional discovery.

When one limits their emotions, such as limiting the expression of the shadowy aspects, or those aspects which we would prefer to suppress, then disaster is bound to occur.

The disaster is not only emotional, but because emotions are so influential and critical to the wellbeing of the body (the mind regulates the body through hormonal responses from emotional input), then the physical health of a person can become compromised. Blood pressure can rise, cortisol levels may elevate, digestion can be affected, sleep patterns may become altered, and the chances for diabetes, heart disease, obesity, etc. can all increase dramatically. With all of the physiological changes that occur, the mind becomes increasingly taxed. The brain is pushed to its limit while trying to maintain homeostasis in an extremely unstable and unbalanced body. Once our vital, inner systems are compromised, then illness has the opportunity to take root and overwhelm the body.

Illness can start in the body and creep into the mind, or can start in the mind and seep into the body. Either way, mental health issues tend to arise.

(Disclaimer: This book is not medical advice. If you feel you have a medical condition which this book touches on, I strongly encourage you to seek professional medical advice and services. This book and its author are not responsible for the medical ideas you gather and substitute for state and federally approved medical advice and services. This book is not intended for the purpose of diagnosis or treatment of any illness or medical condition. Seek professional medical help if you believe you are suffering from a medical condition).

Once mental health issues appear, medications and pills of all shapes and colors are abundantly prescribed. These medications come with radical claims that they will be able to cure all your symptoms by doing the one thing that caused all the discord and illness in the first place: suppress your emotions.

Emotional Discord

When we take medications which suppress our emotions, like antidepressants, we block the connection between our feelings and our mind, affecting our ability to process our emotions and thus altering and affecting our consciousness.

Without consciousness, we are unable to connect and experience the gift of existence: the wonderfully unique relationships experienced through joy and love. Our energy is depleted quickly because we are blocked from the emotional energy which powers our life force.

Western medicine is not bad. Western medicine is not evil. Western medicine is a complementary discipline to Eastern medicine. Medicine is not completely defined within any one discipline. All healing arts hold a truth in medicine. All healing arts contribute a form of medicine which is relevant in one way or another. All healing arts are effective if properly utilized with respect to the illness and its origin.

When it comes to depression, in most cases, what tends to be needed is the balance of complementary energies within ourselves. Depression can come about from the denial or suppression of energies which travel through us in cycles. When we trap energy we basically form a block, preventing the many cycles which flow within and through us from harmonizing. One of the best ways to cure something like depression or bipolar conditions is to express our emotions through a creative medium. Through motion and a creative process, we can find a way to balance the complementary energies within us again.

Creative Creation

The creative process of uniting the masculine energy of potential with the feminine energy of formation can help unblock and balance complementary energies. When enough creative creation has occurred, the two energies work together to harmonize and balance each other. This is the real job of a shaman and healer: to help someone balance their energies or emotions through a creative medium so they may align themselves with the healing process of the cycle of elevation.

A creative medium does not necessarily mean an expression of emotion through a traditional form of art (paintings, dance, poetry, etc.). A creative medium may be the implementation of any new idea or method. It may be calling forth different energies or spirits through some form of ritual. It may be helping a person remember who they are through their past or showing them the potential of what they could be by bringing them into the future. It may be trying something new to rekindle a failing relationship or to overcome an obstacle which is preventing a person from achieving a goal.

The first few creative ideas or processes you try may fail. You may even come to a point where you feel that nothing you do or try is helping you to achieve your goals, whether they be health, wealth, happiness, or some combination of spiritual or material gain. Whatever happens, what is certain is that once you give up, everything will fall away. You may feel like you failed, but really there is no such thing as failure, you just stopped trying. You gave up. When you stop moving toward your meaning and purpose, you fall out of alignment with the cycle of elevation. You need to keep going, you need to keep believing and trying and eventually one of these creative processes will work like magic.

Continue building on this creative magic until the product or outcome you produce becomes irrelevant again. Once your methods are outdated what you create will be of little to no value. When this happens, it doesn't mean that you have become worthless or a failure, it just means that it's time to re-create and re-engage the creative process to engineer something fresh and new, something which brings a magic relevance back into the world.

Mental health issues are a sign or symptom of unbalanced and unregulated emotions. These emotions are usually due to the suppression or denial of some aspect of ourselves which we are unable to accept, understand and integrate. Again, when mental health issues arise, unbalanced and unregulated emotions can be balanced through the creative process—invoking the masculine energy of potential and manifesting an idea through the feminine energy of creation. Complementary energies work together to bring harmony to all of existence.

The way of the warrior is a path of constant re-invention and self-discovery. Through harmonizing the energies within to align with his environment, a warrior is able to grow, adapt, and evolve with the grand cycle of elevation.

Chapter 8

Initiation

Chapter eight starts to integrate our beliefs with the beliefs of others. Here, we take the broken bits of our reality and integrate them with the reality of others to form a deeper understanding of the world. It is the process of integration which broadens our definition of what is possible. These new possibilities expand the way in which we perceive life itself. To come to a deeper understanding, we must mature emotionally. To widen our perception of life we must complete a rite of passage. It is from completing a rite of passage that we come into emotional maturity. From emotional maturity we can achieve a form of self-actualization, the peak of Maslow's hierarchy of needs[1], a pyramid structured toward a transcendent purpose. It is from the summit of Maslow's pyramid that we discover the many pyramids of life.

Emotional Maturity

A rite of passage or an initiation is synonymous with being accepted as a full-fledged member of a community. Within some cultures, a person may earn this right by passing a test or performing and completing some initiation ritual.

---

[1] Maslow's hierarchy of needs explains successive tiers of human needs which can explain human motivation. Needs within the lowest tier must be met prior to moving up through each successive, higher tier, from physiological needs at the bottom, to transcendence at the top.

These rituals may vary from culture to culture, community to community or tribe to tribe. There are many forms of initiation. Some forms of initiation may involve hunting, while other rituals may include a brave leap from a tall cliff into a body of water. Still other forms of initiation can include enduring the bites and stings of a venomous insect colony. The more dangerous forms of initiation can involve some form of combat with other members of the community.

Whatever the initiation or rite of passage may be, they all have one thing in common: emotional maturity. An aspiring member of a particular group needs to develop a certain level of emotional maturity to successfully complete a rite of passage ritual, and thus be acknowledged and accepted as a full-fledged member of that community. There is often a formal ceremony after the initiate passes his or her rite of passage test, where the individual is honored as a new member of the group. It is during the ceremony which the individual inherits an elevated rank along with a certain amount of responsibility and authority.

Hunting as a rite of passage, for example, isn't about the barbaric and mindless slaughter of some poor creature. It's about knowing yourself and knowing your prey. It's about developing and honing your skills as a provider in the most ancient of ways. It's about participating in a timeless tradition with the utmost honor and respect for life and death.

As a true hunter, you must know your strengths and weaknesses, as well as the strengths and weaknesses of your quarry. You must know where to find your prey and be able to anticipate and predict what your target is going to do. You must outwit, out-position and in some instances, overpower your prey. You must also be well versed with your weapon, for the knowledge and skill of your weapon will be paramount in taking down your mark.

In the end, it's not that you proved your superiority by conquering or killing some helpless animal or beast, it's displaying that you are emotionally mature enough to execute all the steps necessary to successfully take down a worthy adversary in the most ethical way possible.

Rite of Passage

What gives me the right to write about these topics?

Everything that I have written has come from the experience of inventing and re-inventing myself over and over again in an attempt, in an ever-perpetuating cycle to expand my understanding of life. My pursuits in physical health, spiritual wellbeing, and mental clarity have in a sense, always been connected to an underlying intention of authentic revelation which would help expose a broader definition of love in some way. Whether my attempts were successful or not, I was determined to remain open. I did not want to close myself off to the possibility of experiencing a new perspective of joy, and thus, my devotion and resiliency has helped me to experience extremes, the far sides of many spectrums. These experiences have helped to unlock and cultivate my genius creativity, the limitless possibility and infinite potential which dwells within us all.

The specifics of my experiences, my achievements, and my suffering are not what has given me the right to speak of these topics and concepts. We all go through the excitement of love and the pain of heartache in some way. We are all gifted with natural abilities and talents, as well as shortcomings, obstacles we must overcome. We all experience those seemingly fleeting moments of pure joy while enduring the seemingly endless search for where we belong and what we are meant to do.

I am not some "chosen one", guru or master; I have simply experienced and overcome enough self-inflicted misery to realize that

I have been making very similar mistakes over and over again. Through the grace of humility, I eventually came to the understanding that my repetitive failures or mistakes were due to the patterns (cognitive behavioral therapy), the routines I chose to incorporate and cycle in my life over and over again.

Only after acknowledging that I was repeating an unproductive cycle that not only prevented me from forming a closer relationship, a more authentic bond with joy and love, but took me further away from them, did I start putting forth the effort to change my habits and my pattern of thinking. I had to shift my perspectives to understand how to align with a meaning, a purpose, which was both attainable and perpetuating.

The acknowledgement and the effort put forth to grow from my failures and limited perspectives prompted help from the guides.

One way the journey toward self-actualization starts is with you. You must accept the toll the journey will take on your emotional endurance and hold yourself accountable for your own life. When you accept responsibility with the resolve to grow, then your guides will activate. The terms should be agreed upon on neutral ground. Contracts which are set in the physical world will tend to favor the physical world. Contracts set in the spirit world will tend to favor the spirit world. Contracts which are sealed in the neutrality of the in-between, the bridge which connects both worlds will tend to benefit both worlds and strengthen the connection which bonds both worlds together.

My path, the realization of my repetitive mistakes and narrow perspectives, paired with my resolve to change and grow is not the only way to receive guidance, but is how my journey into the spirit realms came about. Your path may be completely different. Just know that it will be terribly difficult to reveal and understand your emotional blueprint alone. It is the sum of many experiences, cycles, and guidance from a combination of spirit and physical teachers which will uncover who you are and the path of the middle way. The more the spectrum of existence is expanded upon the clearer the middle way becomes. If you are willing to mature emotionally, humbly acknowledge your shortcomings, and put forth the effort necessary to change and grow, you will begin your rite of passage.

If you accept your situation and put forth the required effort to evolve and elevate, you will find that there are guides not just willing, but eager to help you find your path to meaning and purpose, to help reveal your unique emotional blueprint. Accepting responsibility is paramount for the guides to help you. I have the right to write about these topics because I have earned their guidance through my own accountability. I accepted the responsibility to pass on their knowledge as best I could, hence this book. Through my experience I have come to understand that these are their terms for helping me.

In light of this information, anyone can write about these topics when they have been granted the guidance to do so. In all honesty, the guides are the ones writing this book, and one of the primary messages the guides wish to pass on is that this book is not gospel truth. There are no crystallized doctrines within this text that should be regarded or worshiped as divine law. Take everything within this book as concepts which can be infinitely expanded upon.

Even as I am writing this book, even as I follow the messages as best I can by putting forth the required effort into creating a more harmonious life, I make mistakes. I encounter opposition. I feel emotions of extreme nature. Though the way may be clearer, life is still full of surprises that are meant to be experienced with a sense of awe and wonder, for the mystery and the experience of this mystery in any and all shapes and forms is the gift of life, of existence.

There is no such thing as a perfect life.

The desire for this book is that it be expanded upon by you. You are charged with helping the topics and concepts of this book to evolve and elevate, as long as you are willing to put forth the effort and accept the responsibility for doing so.

Self-Actualization

I hold myself accountable for whatever situation I find myself in because at some point in my life, I asked to be right where I am. I asked for everything that I currently have and everything that I currently don't have.

I am where I am because of what I have chosen to do with the experiences I have been granted. No matter the external circumstances, I have had the freedom to make the conscious decisions which have placed me exactly where I am.

Self-accountability is a way to self-actualization.

Pyramid Scheme

Maslow's hierarchy or pyramid of needs comes to a peak at self-actualization. Self-actualization is described as achieving one's full potential, including creative activities. Even this renowned psychologist's model sets creativity as the pinnacle of human need.

Through creativity we are able to express the light, the gifts, and the joy within us.

When we are able to expand our potential while integrating what is essentially our own, the unique gifts and perspectives within our aspect, we are able to find and to share our purpose. From our purpose we not only achieve self-actualization, but elevation.

Don't worry, this is not the end.

There is no end, just a new beginning—a new cycle to explore and evolve into until we reach elevation again, and again, and again.

Maslow's hierarchy of needs is relative to another hierarchy, the dominance hierarchy. So begins our journey up the great pyramid of needs.

Chapter 9

Hierarchies

Chapter nine takes us into the intricacies of hierarchies. We break down how we can fall and rise in any hierarchy through emotional maturity. There is still some deconstruction going on in chapter nine, but we begin mending reality back together in a way which will broaden our definition of concepts (like joy and love) which will also allow us to expand our vision of what any concept could be.

Alpha and Beta

The dominance hierarchy is a sensitive subject for most because the majority of people in a society fall into the lower levels of the dominance hierarchy. Some people are so low when it comes to this hierarchy model that they live in a place I like to refer to as the "submissive lower level".

To gain a clearer perspective of what it means to live in this lower level status I would like to talk about the monetary hierarchy before we expand upon the dominance hierarchy. The monetary hierarchy provides a framework in which we can reference to from other hierarchies and is a concept that may be a little more familiar to most. Perhaps this model will create a little more clarity.

I Want Money

When it comes to monetary poverty (literally having little to no financial worth), unproductive and destructive decisions tend to outnumber productive and constructive ones. This is not because people experiencing poverty are without morals or values, or because they are inherently lazy or lack the intellect or motivation to change their situation (though laziness and lack of motivation may very well play a role in some cases). Instead, it is often a frame of mind which is difficult to escape.

In my experience of poverty (which is of course relative), the situation itself can feel like a soul-sucking black-hole which can syphon the most beautiful and creative parts of yourself so that only your fear and anxiety remain. Where the venom really dwells is in the awareness. Knowing and understanding the level of poverty you are living in can sting like a thousand hornet pricks.

When poverty bites, the poison can be so daunting, so overwhelming, that it suppresses the creative confidence necessary to not only come up with innovative and productive ideas to change, but also stunts the ability to implement and apply the productive ideas needed to help rise up and out of poverty.

The Fear of being Right

Though those in poverty may experience a state of devastating inadequacy and/or deficiency, they may simultaneously maintain a fear of failure. People in poverty who put forth what they believe to be true effort—who really give it their all—so that they may rise above their situation, can easily abandon their hope and effort by the acknowledgement that they may fail.

There may be an underlying fear that failure would prove to a person who is experiencing poverty that they are actually only worth the desperate situation which they find themselves in. A person who tries and fails to get out of poverty is forced to face one of their worst fears—that they really are insubstantial and/or inadequate and deserve nothing more than the poverty-stricken situation they are in. The thing is, poverty gives people the excuse to say, "I can't do something," and if you believe that excuse, then you are probably right.

The Margin

People in poverty have little room for error. It can almost feel like "game over" if one more traumatic event or failure occurs.

Again, it's the awareness of one's fragile predicament which can often lead to poor choices and/or a reluctance to try something new and innovative to get out of poverty.

The further away from poverty one is, the more productive and constructive his or her choices tend to be and the less substantial the threat of failure becomes. This is because there are adequate resources which form a barrier or cushion to help prevent a catastrophic outcome if he or she were to actually fail.

Creative outlets also tend to rise as poverty is reduced. The feeling of abundance which may come with having enough distance from poverty can bring about the emotional expression of joy, which expands a person's gravity (radius of influence), influencing money and opportunity to be attracted to them.

The obstacles of being at the bottom of the monetary hierarchy translate very well to the obstacles of the dominance hierarchy.

In Demand

When one is positioned high up on the dominance hierarchy, he or she is perceived as more desirable and in demand than others.

Aside from being perceived as desirable and in demand, a person who is high up on the dominance hierarchy positions himself in a way which allows him to gain access to resources that a vast majority of others don't have, yet desire or need. These resources, whether they be goods, services, or knowledge, are all vital elements in solving problems.

The more practical the problem a person can solve, especially in service to others, the higher he or she climbs in the dominance hierarchy.

Serving people and solving problems which plague society is a rite of passage in and of itself.

Helping others ascend Maslow's hierarchy of needs will generate abundance for all.

Helping others advance is where the dominance hierarchy differs from both Maslow's hierarchy of needs and the monetary hierarchy. For both the monetary hierarchy and Maslow's hierarchy of needs is solely focused on the worth or needs of the individual, while the dominance hierarchy is so much more complex that one has to account for the status of his peers and community to rise without force or oppressing others.

Fluctuation

The dominance hierarchy is a strange, shifting model because of how it is measured in relation to the varying aspects or factors which influence it.

For example, one can rise in the dominance hierarchy in one way by achieving success through academia. One of the factors in the dominance hierarchy is how one is measured in accordance to intellectual milestones through the acquisition of degrees and credentials. Higher education tends to open doors to better paying and more secure jobs—as well as a more sophisticated and cultured knowledge of the world and the affairs of men.

Someone who graduates from college with all the honors which can be bestowed upon him can seem at the top of the dominance hierarchy within his peer group, but after graduation, the story changes. As a new chapter begins, that same college graduate with all his honors, has to now apply for potential jobs, placing him at the bottom of the dominance hierarchy.

When people come together in a social gathering, there are many factors which play into who in the group will rise to the top of the dominance hierarchy. In some social settings, education isn't really a factor and can be irrelevant. In every mixed gathering or social platform, the dominance hierarchy shifts and changes in regard to the context of the social setting. For example, the dominance hierarchy at the gym is completely different from the dominance hierarchy at your favorite pub or bar.

If certain social settings become uncomfortable to us, it is usually because we view ourselves at the bottom of the dominance hierarchy in that particular social platform. A great example would be a logger at a habitat conservation expo or a cowboy at a video game convention, assuming these people are not proficient at both.

The criteria necessary to be at the top of the dominance hierarchy in certain social settings may be so uncomfortable that to try and find some common ground with which you can identify or endure may just seem impossible or too painful emotionally to consider attending.

Game of Hormones

One of the major dominance hierarchies is situated around pairing with a mate.

Finding a suitable partner, even for a short time, can prove difficult, especially if you are a male who ranks low on the dominance hierarchy.

Men and women dance around each other, playing games that mimic chess or Guess Who? People play games in hopes to gain the upper hand in a relationship or to prove to the other that he or she is of value, and thus in demand and desirable. For if a person can demonstrate that he is of value and that others desire him, then he will have a significant advantage when choosing who he partners with.

After a while, the majority of men and women become tired trying to out-maneuver one another. Always trying to guess the real identity of a person, or concealing your own in order to position yourself higher in the dominance hierarchy can get old.

The thing is, we can get so caught up in playing games, in ascending the multitude of hierarchies, that we can forget what truly matters.

What truly matters is expanding our emotional blueprint so we may experience life in the most authentic and least restrictive ways as possible while cultivating harmonious relationships which strengthen our bond with all of existence so we can better unite with the source of all creation: joy and love.

Great Shortcomings

Sure, hierarchies are important—they give us structure and a method by which to measure ourselves. We can gauge our strengths and our weaknesses through hierarchies, and then put effort into the places which need to be worked on.

Hierarchies also give people an external coordinate, a tangible and material goal to aim for—we just have to remember to not get lost in the pursuit of acceptance, approval, or applause from others.

The thing that we need to take away from the dominance hierarchy, and many, if not all the other hierarchies out there, is that though we may rise in one hierarchy, there will always be another hierarchy or social situation where we fall short.

I know some highly-educated people who became professors or doctors to try and diminish emotional inadequacy issues.

People with advanced statures have confessed to me that they still feel, for the most part, inadequate. What this has taught me is that just because one attains a high status in a single aspect of the dominance hierarchy, one may still feel quite inadequate in comparison to the broad spectrum which is the dominance hierarchy.

One might even feel inadequate in the aspect of which they have achieved greatness. It is commonly joked that many body builders have emotional inadequacy issues about their bodies. This doesn't mean you shouldn't strive to be fit and pursue external goals and coordinates.

You must definitely act and move toward what captivates you. Just remember to try and mature just as much emotionally in relation to any goal or external coordinate you are striving toward. Rising too fast externally can leave a big gap emotionally which must mature quickly to be able to live up to the newly elevated external expectations. Comparatively, cultivating emotional maturity combined with hard work will raise your external situation as a byproduct.

The physical and emotional aspects of life are complements.

Create a harmonious relationship with the complements in life and you will mature in the ways you are able to experience joy.

If you find yourself in any sort of poverty it can be hard to find many experiences of joy. There is a difference between poverty and choosing to live a simple life. When a person chooses to live a simple life there isn't much lacking as far as needs which are not or haven't been met.

People who choose to live a simple life tend to experience an abundance of joyful experiences, which is one of the main reasons a person would choose to live a simple life in the first place. A person who is experiencing poverty on the other hand, tends to lack experiences of joy due to unmet needs or unfulfilled external coordinates. People who are in poverty tend to experience a form of artificial joy at the bottom of a bottle or through destructive choices and behaviors. As a person emerges from poverty through emotional maturity and hard work, which in turn elevates his external status, his ability to experience joy also expands.

Substances like drugs and alcohol may be one of the only ways a person in poverty can experience an emotion like joy. As a person matures emotionally and takes the necessary steps to bring themselves out of poverty, the artificial joy found in substance abuse can become less satisfying and of little value when compared to the true joy experienced from authentic and harmonious relationships.

Emotional maturity allows a person to rise in status in a variety of hierarchies (dominance, Maslow's, and social for example), expanding the ways a person can experience life with less restriction. A life free from addiction opens the possibility to form the authentic connections which allow a person to expand his emotional blueprint. A person dependent on alcohol who matures emotionally can begin to experience joy through supportive and loving communities, not just through consuming and abusing alcohol (just an example). A person emotionally emerging from poverty and substance abuse can find joy in cultivating healthy relationships, valuing oneself, and the pursuit of constructive and creative outlets.

It is through emotional maturity that we are able to rise in hierarchies and discover joy in so many things. Though we can find joy in just about anything when we rise up and out of poverty, we must be careful not to create dependencies. Substituting a destructive dependency for a less destructive dependency to experience joy is still a dependency.

Self-actualization is attained through harmonious relationships which produce joy. True joy is not experienced from a dependent relationship. Emotional maturity raises our status toward self-actualization, while a given or achieved status may or may not prompt the emotional maturity necessary to live up to the expectations of our given or achieved status.

Depending on the attainment of a goal or external coordinate to deliver you to joy, will only keep you chasing joy. Allow yourself to be open and as least restrictive as possible when connecting with others so you may strengthen your bond with all of creation, just don't be dependent on others to experience the bond you inherently share with all of creation.

When you are not dependent on anything to experience joy, then joy will overflow within you.

Concepts and Definitions

If you are unsure about any of the concepts within this book then take the time to define your version of truth in relation to your version of reality. For example, if you don't agree with the example of love expressed within this book, then seek to understand your definition and perspective of love. Just don't crystallize it into some doctrine or gospel truth which limits your experience of love, or any concept, whether it be love, or joy, or friendship.

Expand upon it.

From your unique version and definition of a concept, like love, explore all the possibilities of what love can be. Through emotional maturity, healthy boundaries, and emotional intelligence broaden your definition of love.

Exploring the possibilities of what love can be elevates your relationship with love and helps reveal the mystery of existence with respect to your boundaries as well as the "mystery's" limitless potential.

Of course we can build ourselves up. Yes, we can rise in the varying levels, the different aspects of any hierarchy, but what does it do for our inner voice?

External coordinates should be the byproduct of cultivating our internal voice, not the other way around; otherwise, we may attain our goals in some vain pursuit before we are even emotionally mature enough to live up to the expectations of our achievements.

If our inner voice isn't ready to deal with the responsibility of our own desires, then our dream can turn into a nightmare. So, heed those famous words yet again, be careful what you wish for—you just might get it.

Great Expectations

Internal coordinates (emotions) which are not yet ready to handle the external coordinates which have somehow been attained pre-maturely, may not quell the feeling of being inadequate and can even cause more emotional turmoil.

For example, when I was only 20 years old, I bought a house. I was able to do this because I went into the lucrative business of sales at 18. I put great effort in the craft of selling not the product, but myself, and I made good money when I began selling cars at a dealership. At 19 I earned my real estate license and was mentored by a broker. I worked hard and was dedicated to achieving my goals and external coordinates. A month or so before my 21st birthday I got the keys to my very own home.

Family and friends were proud. I achieved something which brought me up in the ranks of several hierarchies.

I was expected to behave a certain way with respect to the achievements I had attained. The demands of my status as well as maintaining my lifestyle and image put more pressure on me than I expected.

I became neurotic about my image and raising my status in every hierarchy I could. I chased material success and external coordinates more and more.

Eventually I imploded. My neuroticism got the best of me. I spent too much money, neglected my house, my friends, my family, and eventually, my work.

My inner voice was not ready for what I wished for, even though I worked hard in the beginning to attain it. I was not yet emotionally mature enough to handle all the responsibilities which came with what I wished for.

I went bankrupt at 23.

You see, no matter what external coordinates or achievements we attain, if we are not emotionally ready, then we can become neurotic about the required expectations, so for the most part, we still won't be able to elevate above a certain level in any hierarchy.

Inner Garden

No matter how many grand monuments we erect, if we neglect our inner voice—our inward perception of ourselves that we project out into the world—we will always live in some form of monetary or dominical poverty.

What I have found which tends to both build up our inner voice and raise our status in the dominance hierarchy is authentic creativity manifested into something useful.

Creativity is amazing (assuming you are creative), but that which is recognized to be creative can much of the time appeal to the world as nothing more than a novelty.

To serve a purpose, creativity must be much more than just some trivial thing that presents as shocking or inspiring. To be useful, creativity must be both unique and useful. Creativity must be able to serve a purpose to the majority of people who behold it, should it be accepted as something of purpose and meaning which brings both joy and utility to the tediousness of everyday life. To be useful, creativity must solve a problem or satisfy a need for the masses in a beautiful, clever, and innovative way.

When we are creative in a useful way, a way which impacts the world, or at least provides a practical solution to a group of people, we encourage our inner voice to go beyond external coordinates, beyond personal dreams or desires, beyond expectations, and even beyond neuroticism, to a creative space where we find freedom in service to others.

Don't get me wrong, useful creativity does not have to be a product. Music which touches the soul and influences emotion in a way which unites people is both useful and creative. A painting which widens the perspective of social justice, ethics, spirituality, love, freedom, equality... etc., are both useful and creative. Useful creativity has depth and meaning in both form and purpose.

When we finally come to the conclusion that it's not about us, we are finally ready to earn our rite of passage by serving others. By finding creative ways to help people satisfy their needs and relate to the world through joy and love, we create the opportunity for ourselves and others to rise toward self-actualization.

Creative Block

What if you feel you are simply not creative?

When we share and express our inner aspect, that which is unique to our own emotional blueprint, we uncover our inner voice and expose our creativity. This is important for those who seem to lack creativity or feel they have none.

I have met many people who feel that they are just not creative, but wish they were.

These self-proclaimed creatively sterile people can achieve great levels of external success, but rarely, if ever, contribute something original, extending from within their inner voice. Their approach to life is one of regimen and security, adhering to the recipes laid out before them. Uncreative people can be very mechanical and methodical in the way they approach life.

Though they may seem cheerful and happy at times, many tire from a lack of emotional connection in their lives. They seek out in external relationships that which they so desire within.

Creative Solution

When we cultivate our inner voice, when we are able to extend our unique gift, our emotional blueprint, our genius creativity to the masses, in a way and manner which helps to solve real problems, then we are not only raising our status in the dominance hierarchy, we are unleashing our potential and discovering our purpose.

A creative purpose helps transform and develop our inner voice into a force—a force of influence seated at the top of every hierarchy.

So, for those of you who struggle with creativity, stop looking for external sources of inspiration so much, and look within.

Find yourself.

Finding yourself may sound easy, but I also know it is not.

Ask yourself, honestly, is it worth finally feeling something other than the sterility of repetition? If so, then do whatever it takes to find, uncover, and cultivate your inner voice.

Start with finding the time to explore the things you like, that captivate you on an emotional level, and allow things to develop and evolve. See and feel where things go.

There will be a lot of frustration and failure, but when you find your inner voice, your seat of creativity, you will be overwhelmed with emotion, the kind which lights up your soul—Pure joy.

Chapter 10

The Chase

Chapter ten is about choosing the pieces we incorporate back into our lives. In chapter nine, we began mending the broken pieces of our reality back together. Here, in chapter ten, we learn to understand the pieces which will help us move toward our meaning and purpose, as well as the pieces that may prevent us from moving all together. There are pieces which will have us chasing artificial coordinates and spending our valuable time and energy on excess if we choose to keep them.

Chapter ten is about learning—learning not to chase, and instead, learning to strip away the unessential. We will also learn about the artificial systems which sustain our way of life. Ultimately, we can remain stuck in the dream or integration stage if we ignorantly refuse to learn about the systems and institutions which support the artificial world we have decided to create and live in.

Ultimately, we will learn that we don't have to be held captive in the realities which others have created if we learn to integrate our reality with the artificial and organic realities of the collective consciousness of the world.

My Best Life

What is your ideal life?

Many people subscribe to the idea of cheap thrills and no

obligations as part of the recipe for their best life. I was one of those people who believed that the pleasure and gratification required for my best life would only be obtained through any path which led me to the least amount of responsibility as possible.

The pursuit of pleasure and gratification isn't all bad, but the sole pursuit of gratification without regard for your physical and emotional health, as well as the wellbeing of others, can lead to impulsive behavior motivated by the selfish desires for instant gratification.

Instant gratification can mask our purpose and ability to experience true love and joy. If our purpose is overshadowed by the selfish illusion of pleasure above all, the pursuit of instant gratification can lead to the collapse of our internal systems. Our natural alignment with the cycle of elevation and ourselves can be severely compromised.

I remember I hated eating as a kid. I thought it was a ridiculous ritual which took too long and wasted precious play time. So, of course I would forgo eating for as long as possible and refuse the nutritious meals and snacks my mother would prepare.

Then it would happen. My whole world would collapse as my stomach protested for the nourishment and nutrition it needed to continue to provide me with energy. Hunger would eventually overwhelm my system, and my poor meager mind, my beautiful little brain, couldn't cope with the urgent, emotional sensations unleashed by my stomach.

I would crash. Fun, happiness and joy were no longer of any importance to me because my needs were not met. I had no one to blame but myself, though I would still project my anger and frustration onto other people, mainly my mom.

If our needs aren't being met, if we forgo our obligations to cultivate and maintain wellbeing in ourselves and each other, no matter how much joy, fun, and happiness we are experiencing, we are not living our best life.

Our "best life" cannot be realized while we are in denial or in conflict with the natural cycle of our systems or the natural cycle of nature. The pursuit of any great goal, the motivation and energy behind any endeavor, must be balanced and in align with the natural cycles of life.

There is night and there is day, a time for activity and a time for rest. We cannot thrive living in either extreme. There must be a balance, a cycle which allows our emotions to accept, understand, integrate, and elevate. When we forgo our needs, when we try and dismiss our obligations, we disrupt our cycle and the possibility of our best life.

The other side to this story is that people tend to confuse joy and happiness with pleasure. People want to feel pleasure because it's such an amazing, euphoric, and fantastic feeling. Whatever satisfies a person's emotions, whatever gives him or her a sense of pleasure or instant gratification, can be mistaken for joy and happiness.

True joy and happiness are achieved and experienced through satisfying needs and fulfilling obligations—the responsibilities necessary to sustain and maintain life within ourselves as well as our family or community.

In a family or community, hardship as well as joy can be shared and experienced by everyone. Working together helps the whole group progress in the cycle of elevation.

There is a price for everything.

For every action there is an equal and complementary reaction.

Life is not free.

Put yourself in the shoes of any wild creature. Whether you're a plant or animal, predator or prey, once you begin your journey in life, you are expected to endure in one way or another.

The price for life is ENDURANCE.

The cost to live is emotional endurance.

When we feel we can endure no more, "poof," we go. Perhaps our beloved partner passes away. Maybe we are suffering too much pain from a traumatic event. Whatever it may be, if life feels too overwhelming, if we can't bear to live anymore because we feel we have lost our meaning, our connection with existence and have suffered too much, when we feel like our emotional endurance has reached its absolute limit, we let go of our life force. When we are done dealing with all the stress and pain of life, when our emotional endurance runs out, we die.

I contrast, when we say someone is strong, or that he or she is a fighter, what we are referencing to in regard to this person is his or her emotional endurance—the emotional fortitude to keep going and to keep LIVING.

It may seem like humans were made to suffer, but life isn't all about paying the fee of emotional endurance. The silver lining of fulfilling our obligations and responsibilities is celebration. We must celebrate our emotional endurance, our connection with nature, our genius creativity, our achievements, as well as the gift of life itself.

More often than not, celebration may be both short and bittersweet. This is because enlightenment and the cycle of elevation requires one to keep enduring, to keep expanding toward a transcendent purpose.

We satisfy needs and achieve goals only to strive for progress in other areas of our lives, as well as aspects which are ephemeral or infinite.

As we expand our potential by extending our limitations, when we start to fill in the gaps of who we are, then we can begin to understand our true potential and purpose.

When we live in alignment with our potential and purpose, we are able to accomplish more as well as inspire and motivate a great number of people. We can take on seemingly impossible projects while maintaining a harmonious balance through it all.

When we are able to maintain a harmonious balance in pursuit of our purpose, we have basically completed our rite of passage. We can venture fourth into the community as full-fledged members of society.

Ultimately, we will be able to help the world evolve and elevate through the development of our own emotional maturity and healthy boundaries.

We must find our own way into emotional maturity, and once attained, must not impose our path onto others as the only means to achieve emotional maturity.

If we respect the unique paths of others, we can serve as guides. We may help others find their own extraordinary path to emotional maturity and enlightenment.

We must lead by example. We must demonstrate to others how to cultivate symbiotic relationships with ourselves, our surroundings, and one another.

The process of leading by example while respecting the paths of others may be tedious in effort and require a mature emotional blueprint so one can be both firm and sensitive to the needs and desires of others. Being a guide requires patience. Being a guide requires the acceptance, understanding, and integration of all aspects which align with the cycle of elevation.

Alignment produces a joyful experience which is held together by the magnetic force of love. Only when one finds joy and love in anything and everything do the external coordinates of any desire fall away as irrelevant illusions, for you find yourself surrounded with the joy and love you so desperately sought through the journey itself.

It is the whole journey, the entire process of life in which joy and love should be experienced—especially when fulfilling obligations and satisfying needs become difficult. This is what is meant by "a labor of love."

No matter what stage you find yourself at in life, if you can achieve joy and happiness in all things, you are living your best life.

Excess

I am not implying that you should add stress or obligations to your life in order to achieve emotional maturity, a maturity which will blossom into meaning and purpose.

Think of what is essential, what is necessary—then strip away the excess.

Adding unnecessary elements to your life doesn't make you more worthy or better deserving of joy and love than someone who chooses to minimize responsibility. Sometimes people add things to replace something which they lost or because they don't know how to spend their time. What they are really doing is searching for a purpose. Not all endeavors help achieve a relationship with purpose, love, or joy, but rather drains vital energy. Excess makes you work harder to maintain material possessions and artificial relationships. Accumulating things or responsibilities doesn't move you any closer to emotional maturity.

Adding one selfish illusion on top of another drains the energy and resources necessary for you to discover and reveal the beauty of your true potential.

A sculptor doesn't add clay to his work—rather, he strips away the nonsense, the unessential, until the truth of his art is revealed.

Balance

The duality or duplicity of these lessons can be confusing.

On one hand, you mustn't allow yourself to fall victim to the pursuit and illusion of pleasure, but on the other hand, you mustn't let work overtake your life.

The paradox is part of the beauty of it all.

You must have ample experience from the patterns of the past in order to hone the skills and insight necessary to navigate the present. While navigating the present you must also pay attention to the emerging patterns which destiny is revealing to you. These revelations help you to understand what the future may or may not bring so you can make adjustments to your trajectory.

Navigating the ocean of life requires a balanced emotional blueprint.

A balanced emotional blueprint requires both emotional intelligence and healthy boundaries to achieve emotional maturity.

Balance is necessary both internally and externally in life and your inner voice is the bridge which connects you to both of these worlds.

Captivity

If we are unable to achieve balance and come into emotional maturity we will not be able to navigate the sea of life. If we are unable to navigate the sea of life then we may never be able to locate the shores of our purpose. Our voyage in this world will seem a lost and vulnerable expedition. Instead of creatively sculpting our potential and expressing the art which our unique emotional blueprint has to offer, we become desperate refugees adrift in the ocean of life.

Unable to fathom the endless possibility of life, we cling to whatever or whomever claims to have the best interpretation of it all. Our naivety and uncertainty can lead us to be taken advantage of by institutions and systems who lure us in with what we desire most—a fool proof recipe which will bring joy, love, and purpose to our lives.

We yearn for answers, but we ask the wrong questions. If we are stuck asking the wrong questions, the answers we seek will never be revealed.

What's worse is that the wrong questions can be grafted into our blueprint by institutions who claim they have all the answers. When prefabricated questions are drafted for us and packaged with premade conclusions, we can be persuaded to accept artificial answers.

Once we believe in the false reality constructed by the irrelevant questions and artificial answers supplied to us, we are primed to willingly pledge our allegiance to whomever or whatever declares they will not just provide us with our purpose, but take care of us.

It is at this moment—when we stop asking questions and renounce our responsibility and accountability for the answers we seek, answers which only we can authenticate in our quest to revel our purpose—that we lose our freedom and give up our emotional blueprint. Our emotions and our inner voice become silenced as we submit to captivity, surrendering our wildness and succumbing to the parameters and limits set forth before us.

Although institutions can amplify illusion, we cannot blame them for our current situation or even the state of the world. Institutions operate because people allow them to through the surrender of their own power. Institutions survive by giving people what they desire. If we are to change the institution, we need to change what we desire.

It all boils down to supply and demand. If we want a better world, if we want substance and value and purpose, then we must desire it. If the masses demand it, institutions will be forced to change to find a way to supply it. If you believe institutions have kept you from progressing in life, then you have surrendered to them.

Rather than giving in to defeat, you can be proactive by studying the institutions and social systems which you claim are suffocating your growth. Educate yourself as unbiasedly as possible instead of protesting without offering a solution which is both creative and practical.

Learn how institutions work instead of assuming what they do. When you understand how a system actually operates, you can use it to help you progress. Though the system may be flawed in many ways, you might find that it isn't as bad as you originally thought.

Understanding and using systems (artificial or organic) to help you elevate will also help you to elevate the system itself.

Stage 4: Winter-Hibernation-Night-Elevation

Welcome to stage four: elevation. Congratulations, you have come to a place where new possibilities and enchantments are woven into the magic of existence itself. Winter can cover the land in white, a canvas reflecting all colors of light which fill the world with new possibilities. Stage four is much like the chrysalis of a caterpillar. After we have successfully integrated our reality with the realities of others (which allow us to expand our emotional blueprint and reach deeper into the collective consciousness of the world), we must fully absorb our new image through rest. Night processes and transforms our newly formed prototype of reality into a fully operational version of reality, much like how the color black absorbs and transforms light energy into heat energy, which is then used as an element to help manifest a new reality. Elevation is a cycle which perpetuates the transformation of energy into new possibilities.

Chapter 11

The Puzzle of Progress

Chapter eleven is about the new self and the understanding of how to elevate into a new form and image. Progress can be confusing. To help us understand progress, and even the *joy* of progress, we must understand the fundamentals of energy and emotion. From the fundamental understanding of energy and emotion we can come to better understand the many concepts which constitute life.

This section is much longer than previous chapters and by comparison, is filled with abstract theories the likes of which you may get lost in. If you find you are having trouble with any of the concepts presented in this section, please feel free to skip around the difficult areas and delve into the places which enchant you. Please come back to the harder parts when you are ready. Sometimes, after more experience or further reading, a difficult concept will transform like magic into something as brilliant and intuitive as the experience of joy.

Emotional maturity

True progress comes from emotionally maturing to a point where we don't need to validate ourselves to others, for we are doing the things we know we are meant to do, and we are sharing the divine gift we are born with—the gift which is coded within our emotional blueprint.

Many of us don't know or haven't revealed our emotional blueprint because we're too busy trying to acquire external validation for our existence. External validation can make it seem as if we have found our meaning and purpose, but I am not here to validate you and you are not here to validate me. We are here to validate ourselves through a healthy relationship with all of existence. We often try to fit the wrong pieces—pieces which don't even belong—into the puzzle of our purpose and existence, which actually prevents us from emotionally maturing. Once our emotional blueprint blooms into a maturity which aligns with our own personal progression, our path will not need to be explained. We will not have to defend the pieces we chose to fit into our puzzle of purpose nor will our self-esteem require validation by others. Best of all, who are as a person will definitely not need to be proven by attaining any external coordinate.

The puzzle of progress—the path toward a mature emotional blueprint—is filled with a kind of awareness which helps us assimilate an understanding of our true meaning and purpose: Self-actualization.

E*motion* $= \text{Mc}^2$

The concept of masculine and feminine energies has been explored far longer than humans have been conscious, for these energies are as old as time itself. In ancient civilizations, the masculine and the feminine energies were symbolized by the sun and the moon, respectively. These masculine and feminine symbols have persisted into today's age.

The concepts you are about to read are not new. Everything in this book has been conveyed in some shape or form within some culture, some religion, or some spiritual practice. However, what I am about to relay may push some boundaries. I have written about it somewhat ambiguously throughout the book, but for all intents and purposes, I would like to make it completely clear.

Everything is energy and energy is vibration or frequency.

So then, what is frequency and why is understanding frequency even relevant or useful (and what does this have to do with masculine and feminine energies)?

The answer to what frequency is and why this knowledge is useful can be somewhat explained with the help of Einstein's theory of relativity.

There are several variations of Einstein's theory of relativity, but the two variations of the equations we will explore are:

1. $E=Mc^2$, where E is used to represent total energy (kinetic plus potential), a capital "M" is used to represent mass at rest plus the extra mass gained when moving (with both kinetic and potential energy), and c^2 is the speed of light squared; and

2. $E_0=mc^2$, where E_0 is used to represent potential energy, a lowercase "m" is used to represent mass at rest (with potential energy), and c^2 is the speed of light squared.

We will explore the variation of Einstein's equation with the "E" and the capital "M" first, or $E=Mc^2$, to understand how total energy is relative to the total emotional experience.

The equation will be used to help reveal the emotional blueprint (not completely, as the mystery expands with every revelation) rather than the laws of physics, for what will be uncovered within this chapter is how energy and emotion are interchangeable in a similar way Einstein's theory of relativity expresses how mass and energy are interchangeable. We will also discover the root of masculine and feminine energy.

Theories can help reveal the puzzle of progress. Some theories can seem to make the puzzle of progress more confusing. My hope is that this theory helps to reveal the puzzle of progress.

I tried to convey this theory which was revealed to me by my guides as best I could. As you read it, if you wish to read it, remember that theories are not defined as proof of absolute truth, theories are a proposed system which may better explain why and how things work. It is my belief that someone with a greater understanding of physics and metaphysics will be able to expand upon this theory to grant us all more insight into the role emotions play within existence itself.

$E=Mc2$

The "E" in $E=Mc^2$ can be substituted for emotion because energy is frequency and frequency at its root, its core, is emotion.

Energy is emotion.

Here is the explanation:

E = Total emotion, kinetic plus potential emotion. Kinetic is the experience of emotion, while potential is the possibility of emotion. For example, if we use love to represent "E," then "E" would be the total love, or the emotional experience of love plus the potential of love itself, for the emotional experience of love can be stimulated far beyond the intensity of love we are experiencing at any given moment.

We can use emotion to represent "E" because like energy, emotion is measured through frequency or vibration. Every emotion has a corresponding frequency, just as all energy has a corresponding frequency. Excitement has a particular frequency which reads differently from the frequency of sadness, just as wave frequency is related to wave energy. Waves are traveling energy. Higher frequency waves contain more energy (or emotion) while lower frequency waves contain less energy (or emotion).

At the quantum level, mass is always vibrating or expressing some frequency. Therefore, everything is energy, and energy (emotion) is transformed through the influence of other forms or aspects of energy (emotion).

The physical mass of an object in physics is a form of energy and is why the "M," or mass, is also emotion.

Einstein's general theory of relativity expresses that mass and energy can be changed into each other. However, mass and energy are not equal, they are proportional.

Equal would refer to mass and energy as being the same in all respects, while proportional refers to mass and energy in a direct relation arithmetically. Mass and energy are proportional to one another because of a constant in the universe: the speed of light.

The speed of light influences and takes energy to a whole new level. If the speed of light is a constant, then energy and mass will be proportional. The larger the mass, the larger the energy, but they are not equal. Mass is much smaller than the energy, because mass (mass at rest plus the extra mass gained while moving) needs to be multiplied by a constant, the speed of light in a vacuum squared, to equal the total energy, kinetic plus potential. Just about any amount of mass multiplied by the speed of light in a vacuum squared produces an astronomical number. This astronomical number represents the total energy, kinetic plus potential, of a mass.

The potential for energy is essentially limitless, and like energy, the potential for any emotion is essentially limitless. This is how energy and emotion can be interchanged; not as proportional, but equal. The explanation of light in Einstein's theory of relativity will demonstrate how energy and emotion are equal.

In physics, light, or more specifically, the speed of light, is somewhat of a Holy Grail. It is no wonder that Einstein used not just the speed of light in his equation, but the speed of light in a vacuum, so there would be nothing to interfere with the speed of light.

Einstein goes even further with light in his equation and squares the already awesome number of the speed of light.

It may be arguable that light is responsible for not just existence but life itself. The light (or heat) of a sun, or star, is required for all known life to exist, and the gravity of a star is responsible for holding planets in orbit around its life-giving warmth and light.

Some stars (the likes of which are much bigger than our sun) can explode into a supernova before collapsing into a black hole. A supernova is what is needed to generate the elements needed to create life. Even at the end of light, there is potential for life.

Through the emotional blueprint, light is represented as joy. Just as the field between infrared and ultraviolet represent the spectrum of light, the totality of emotion, the field between complementary emotions—like fear and love—represent the spectrum of joy.

Infrared and ultraviolet are forms of light which vary in frequency, just as fear and love are forms of joy which vary in frequency. Again, excitement has a particular frequency which reads differently from the frequency of sadness. All emotions are aspects of joy as all waves of light (whether they are yellow waves, infrared waves, or ultraviolet waves) are aspects of light. A frequency of emotion corresponds to a frequency of light, just as a frequency of light corresponds to a frequency of emotion. Every frequency of light in the spectrum of light corresponds with a frequency of emotion in the spectrum of emotion. Therefore, the spectrum of light encompasses all feelings of emotion, as the spectrum of emotion encompasses every hue of light. In the end, everything is energy and energy is emotion. To go even further, all energy is a form of light as all emotion is a form of joy.

Joy is at the core, the center of all extreme emotions, just like the equatorial regions of our planet is the center of biodiversity. All life, all creation springs and expands from these equatorial regions, just as all of existence springs and expands from the center of emotion: joy.

In metaphysics, joy, or more specifically, the attainment of joy is somewhat of a Holy Grail. It is no wonder that Aristotle spent most of his life philosophizing about a Greek version of joy called, *Eudaimonia*. For Aristotle, Eudaimonia isn't a novel emotion like fun or happiness. Eudaimonia is a form of joy which encompasses the totality of one's life. This joy is not something which can be gained or lost in a matter of moments, like pleasurable experiences. Joy is more like the transcendent value of life itself.

In physics, the speed of light in a vacuum is recognized as a universal constant. In metaphysics, the power of joy (along with the power of suffering) are among the constants. What the emotional blueprint is declaring is that all emotions are an aspect of joy, and thus, suffering is just an aspect of joy. Joy is a universal constant just as the speed of light is a universal constant.

In Einstein's general theory of relativity, energy is equal to mass times the speed of light squared.

Why is light squared? The reason light is squared is that the energy of motion, or kinetic energy, is proportional to mass. The easiest way I can think of to describe the relationship of kinetic energy to mass is the acceleration of an object. When an object picks up speed, or accelerates, the kinetic energy of the object increases in relation to the speed of the object squared. The best example I came across to illustrate this phenomena is the relation of an accelerating car to its breaking distance. In a hypothetical controlled environment, while driving an average car, if you double your speed, the breaking distance becomes four times longer. Basically, the force needed to stop the vehicle is equal to the speed of the vehicle squared, or the breaking distance is equal to the speed squared.

The speed of light is an enormous number. The speed of light squared is a monumental number and illuminates how even the smallest bit of matter can contain a colossal amount of energy. If we took a gram of matter, a liquid for example, like water (the four states of matter are: gas, liquid, solid, plasma) and transformed its entire mass into pure energy using the formula, $E=mc^2$, the energy released would translate to the equivalent of about 20,000 tons of dynamite exploding. This is how a tiny amount of plutonium or uranium can create what is probably the most feared of all weapons: a nuclear bomb.

The formula $E=mc^2$, Einstein's general theory of relativity has given rise to numerous technologic achievements. Einstein's equation helped us to better understand our nearest star, the sun, how to harness nuclear energy, and opened the door to medical marvels like nuclear medicine. Einstein's formula illustrates how energy and matter are not just interchangeable, they are one.

Einstein's general theory of relativity is now opening the door to understand energy in a completely new way: as emotion.

In his equation, Einstein uses the speed of light as a multiplier to find the total energy, kinetic plus potential energy, of a physical mass. More-so, Einstein uses the speed of light in a vacuum so nothing can act upon or influence the speed of light in any way. According to the emotional blueprint, the speed of light translates to time (Einstein's general theory of relativity even expresses that as one nears the speed of light, time drops to zero), and time translates to power. Time and power are used in later examples, but basically, if you go too fast, time ceases to exist. You can have all the energy in the universe, but without time, there is no power, hence why time equals power.

Joy is subject to influence just as light is. Rather than putting joy in a theoretical vacuum, joy may be expressed as it was at the beginning of time, the moment of existence, the big bang itself. Therefore, the new equation uses the power of pure joy squared as a multiplier to find the total emotion, potential plus experienced emotion. Whatever this monumental number is, it is equivalent to the speed of light in a vacuum squared.

The reason pure joy is squared is that *experienced emotion*, or the emotional experience, is proportional to the emotion at rest with the extra emotion gained while being experienced. When you stimulate an emotion, the emotional experience amplifies in relation to the intensity of the emotion squared. You'll find an excellent example of this in any romantic experience—like the speed and braking distance example of a car in relation to mass and kinetic energy—if an emotion is doubled in intensity (like love), the emotional effort necessary to reset love and bring the emotional experience back to an emotion at rest is multiplied by its intensity, so the rest state is equal to the intensity of the emotion squared.

The amplification of an emotion like love (to the power of pure joy squared) is why some people never heal from a broken heart, or why there is a saying that love conquers all. This is true of all emotions, not just love. When we focus on stimulating an emotion or belief to an extreme intensity, there isn't much that can stand in our way.

The amplification of an emotion can also blaze a path of destruction. If I harm someone in some way, the energy or emotion used to wrong the person doesn't just stop or go away. The energy of a single act (which is always caused by emotion) can take on momentum. If I wrong a person, I create the potential for an emotional response (whether the person I wronged chooses to act after they have reacted to the potentially destructive emotion is their choice) which may return to me with more intensity or be passed on to someone else with more intensity. Sometimes, the wrong which was inflicted on a person is held within and amplified. A person can hold onto this emotion intensifying it to an unforgivable magnitude. This is the reason why sins can produce so much guilt or require so much penance, and why the karma of one life can take many lives to atone for.

In comparison, the joy, or transcendent value of one life, can make such an impact that the whole world can be influenced to progress toward elevation. Mother Theresa is a wonderful example of how the emotional energy of a single life can radiate so potently. Mother Theresa existed to help give life to others. Her purpose was in alignment with the grand cycle of the universe. The energy within a single purpose can help the world to heal and come together. The joy and love of just one person can affect the collective consciousness of existence.

Emotion is more powerful than we tend to acknowledge. Love, fear and any emotion extending beyond or between these two emotions can create just as much energy as a massive atomic explosion if expressed or converted into pure emotion.

Joy is the light of life.

All energy translates or transmits as some form of vibration or frequency, and that frequency, in turn, is coded with some aspect of emotion. Emotion isn't just something we feel. Everything we see, experience, and interact with is actually a form of emotion, including you and me.

Energy (emotion) influences all the mass at rest (emotion at rest), all objects (all emotions) in existence, producing the potential for infinite interactions to occur. In turn, these infinite interactions produce the possibility for endless energy (emotional) transformations. Existence depends on infinite potential. Existence isn't governed by logic, nor is it ruled by energy (emotion). Existence is the byproduct of potential and kinetic energy (potential and experienced emotion) coming together and interacting in a way which creates motion (experience) in any and all variants. Existence isn't order or chaos, existence is a braided variant of the two in any and all possible forms.

$$E_0 = mc^2$$

Now let's take a look at the variation of Einstein's equation

$E_0 = mc^2$, where the "E_0" is used to represent total potential energy of "m," a mass at rest (with potential energy), in relation to a constant in the universe, "c^2," the speed of light in a vacuum squared.

This variation of Einstein's equation when related to emotion can help us understand the total *potential* emotional experience of an emotion at rest (with potential emotion) in relation to a constant in the universe, the power of pure joy squared.

Let's say I heard an announcement that my favorite book was going to be turned into a movie. Let's say I wanted to see the movie even though I knew how difficult it would be to make a movie better than the book. The thing is, I am already emotionally invested in the book, so for better or for worse, I am committed to see the movie when it's released.

Before I see the movie, the potential emotional experience within me is waiting to be released. There are infinite scenarios which could follow. I could love the movie, I could hate the movie, I could be captivated by the visual effects, I could be appalled by the acting, etc. There are so many possibilities for the movie to release an emotional experience within me.

The total potential emotional experience is equal to the emotion at rest (with potential) which may be released, multiplied by a constant in the universe, the power of pure joy squared.

The total potential emotional experience could be anything. I could be completely disappointed, utterly swept away, or anything beyond or between these emotions. It is the possibility that I could be completely surprised and overwhelmed with extreme emotions which compels the potential emotional experience within me to amplify in relation to the power of pure joy squared (basically my expectations grow) while I eagerly anticipate the release of the movie.

It's the hope of a complete and utter emotional release which draws my attention toward the movie (emotion at rest with potential emotion), for the movie represents the possibility for an emotional experience which may exceed all my expectations. This potential emotional experience vibrates inside of me with such a tenacious frequency that there would be almost nothing which would prevent me from attending the premier of the movie.

Until this potential emotion is set free (whether it turns out to be disappointment or amazement), I am infinitely unsatisfied. I remain unfulfilled until the potential emotion within me is liberated and experienced or until a new potential emotion (or energy) replaces the potential emotion within me.

The more our potential emotions are stimulated toward a potential emotional experience, the more intense the total potential emotional experience becomes in relation to the power of pure joy squared. Our hope of the total potential emotional experience can grow to colossal proportions. This is how our expectations can far exceed our actual experiences. Reality tends to always fall short of our hopes and dreams. It is the inability to accept what is, and establish a relationship with how things are, which can keep us pursuing unhealthy cycles. Left unfulfilled, we dream of an emotional experience that would satisfy all the unrealistic expectations within us. Unrealistic expectations would have us pursue illusions which divorce us from reality.

Dream of a way to expand the ability in which joy and love can be experienced, and no—one-experience—will have the authority to transform hope into despair or dreams into nightmares.

Dream in relation with, the reality of how things are, and the hope for some divine experience will transform into a connection with the joy and love which satisfies all desires.

Understanding the reality of how things are, is part of the puzzle of progress. So, let us talk about the reality of physics and metaphysics in relation to the masculine and feminine energies.

Mass at rest (or energy at rest) is simply potential motion (or potential emotion) waiting to happen, like an apple delicately dangling from a tree branch.

An apple hanging from a tree has potential, the energy or emotion acting upon the apple (or object) is gravity (or love). Before the mass of the apple is overwhelmed by gravity and falls, the apple is said to have potential energy (or emotion). At this point, anything can happen to the apple. Yes, the apple has the potential to fall, but it may also get plucked by a hungry mammal, carried off by a bird, blown away by a storm, or eaten on the branch by a very hungry caterpillar.

There is so much potential energy, or emotion, which can act upon the apple and release its energy, or emotion. The apple is filled with so much potential.

Potential energy, potential emotion, is masculine energy. Masculine energy is the possibility for energy or emotion to be released in some way or form.

Once released, masculine energy transforms into an experience, or motion. Experienced emotion is a form of motion, and motion is kinetic energy, which is feminine energy.

When potential energy is released, when an event occurs, whether it be an apple falling from a tree or two people meeting, the totality of a potential emotional experience occurs "E_0." This totality of a potential emotional experience, whether it be gravity pulling the apple off the tree or love pulling two people together, is just a release and transformation of energy from potential to kinetic, potential emotion to experienced emotion, or masculine to feminine energy.

Masculine energy, potential energy, and potential emotion, are all the same thing.

Feminine energy, kinetic energy, and an emotional experience are all the same thing.

Masculine or potential energy is a potential emotion waiting to be transformed by feminine or kinetic energy so the totality of a potential emotional experience relative to the power of pure joy squared can occur.

Every physical event or occurrence has emotion behind it. When you hold an object, it has the potential to fall. When you drop an object, it not only releases the potential energy into kinetic energy (masculine to feminine) but it releases the total potential emotional experience, which will affect the next object it interacts with. If there is a conscious observer, the release of a total potential emotional experience will activate an emotional response.

What if there's no observer? Everything is connected. Even if there is no one to observe the release of a total potential emotional experience, it doesn't mean that it didn't happen. If there is no observer it doesn't mean that energy, or emotion, wasn't released and transformed. The world has been covered in ice. Dinosaurs did roam the Earth. Many terrible and magnificent things happened before humans were here to observe and catalog them, and many more amazing things will continue to occur after we are gone.

Mass acts upon mass, energy acts upon energy, emotion acts upon emotion, releasing a transformation of interchangeable energies which produce the potential for endless emotional experiences and the limitless possibilities for existence itself. Energy is physics, emotion is metaphysics, both of which are derived in some way, shape, or form from the masculine and feminine energies.

Between Emotions and the Mind

It has been said before that existence itself can very well be the byproduct of our consciousness.

What has been revealed to me is that consciousness does not

dwell in some secret area of the mind, but lives and thrives as energy (potential as well as other kinds of energy) within our emotions.

The mind—our beautiful, highly evolved mind—processes emotion (just like a computer processes data), transforming what we feel into reality. When a biostructure (like the human body) is able to unite a highly evolved intellect with a highly elevated emotional core (or gut), consciousness is born. Reality is the byproduct of our consciousness.

The varying relationships between emotion and intellect among people create unique emotional blueprints. This diversity of emotional blueprints make up the collective human consciousness, similarly to how the millions and billions of unique organisms make up the eco-system which supports life on earth. If one organism or system begins to dominate the earth, then the whole eco-system will be affected. Likewise, if a particular concept, emotion, or mindset manages to monopolize the majority of emotional blueprints, then the collective consciousness of the world will be affected.

We literally project our perception of the world through how we process our emotions. The world can be anything we want. If we want the world to be a beautiful and creative place, then we project that aspect through how we feel—we project our happiness and our understanding or belief of what beauty and creativity is to us onto our reality.

The ability to make life anything we want is the gift and the curse of our emotional blueprint.

All versions of reality are valid.

Reality isn't logic alone—reality is the combination of logic (math) and emotion (potential or energy), just as existence isn't feminine energy alone—existence is the combination of masculine and feminine energies. Everything is a combination of complements in some variant.

Within any reality, logic cannot exist by itself—otherwise, potential is denied. Life cannot exist in a purely robotic way because it would be denied the emotion necessary to experience the connection with all of existence. Life also cannot exist purely within the chaos of emotion, for there wouldn't be any structure, there wouldn't be anything to hold reality together. Reality ebbs and flows. Although reality may seem constant or predictable, the potential for anything to occur *is possible* even if the probability for an extreme event is incredibly small. As we try to balance logic and emotion, as we ebb and flow through what is actually happening, we create a version of reality.

Reality exists between fantasy (chaos/emotions) and reality (structure/the mind).

Collective Consciousness

Quantum objects are the building blocks of existence itself and in quantum mechanics, anything and everything is possible. Since anything is possible in quantum mechanics—quantum mechanics is composed of emotion (energy) and structure (math)—all versions of reality are valid.

What you feel to be the truth and what I feel to be the truth can be different and even divorced from the actual truth, but this doesn't invalidate what you *feel* or what I *feel* to be the truth. We all live within our own dimensions of reality.

Each individual contributes his or her own unique perspective of reality to the potential of existence. The world is composed of the collective consciousness, the emotional blueprints of all of humanity. Thus, the reality and state of the world is a perception of the collective human consciousness.

When we focus on what's within—when we look inward to see

how we can mature, grow, and progress in the cycle of elevation—we expand the potential of the collective human consciousness. Expanding the potential of the collective human consciousness influences and persuades the world to evolve and elevate.

Start with yourself and grow your influence if you wish to make a difference in the world.

The Architecture of Objective Reality and Experience

The general shapes and colors of things are a broad representation of emotion.

The details—the architecture and design of things—are a representation of math, which we will delve deeper into when we talk about *The Art of Existence.*

The color (the light which isn't absorbed but is reflected back) is a representation of the dominant aspect of an entity. For example, the dominant aspect of a plant may be green, or the frequency of green which is the color the plant reflects so our eyes are able to perceive the plant as green.

In addition to the dominant aspect which an entity generally embodies, the emotional aspect of light which an entity emits at any one time may change. For example: joy, love, anger, and fear may cycle through an entity and influence the color being emitted.

An experience is transformed and emitted as emotion. Through the experience of interaction (absorption), a change or transformation occurs (such as the excitation of molecules), and energy is emitted as a different color (or wavelength). This is the process of fluorescence: absorption, transformation, and emission. This is what happens when an entity experiences an emotion.

The aspect of light an entity is emitting is in direct correlation with the frequency in which a form of creation operates and relates with its surroundings. A solid has a definite shape and volume. A solid is an aspect of light whose particles are tightly packed and have a strong enough bond between one another that they cannot move freely, they can only vibrate. A solid is a state of matter which relates to its surroundings through a relatively stable and definite form.

A liquid has no shape but retains nearly a constant volume. A liquid is an aspect of light whose particles are loosely packed with a kind of bond which allows the structure to be mobile. A liquid is a state of matter which relates to its surroundings through flow.

A gas is free from shape or volume unless held in a container. A gas is an aspect of light whose particles have a very weak bond, or no bond at all, allowing it to move quickly and freely as well as expand or be compressed. A gas is a state of matter which relates to its surroundings through the freedom of movement, expanding and compressing into any space.

Plasma, the fourth state of matter is an aspect of light similar to a gas, but with charged particles. This means plasma can conduct electricity and produce magnetic fields of various strengths. Plasma is a state of matter which relates to its surroundings through electricity and magnetism, which mean waves become an important factor when understanding the relationship or interaction of plasma with its environment. Wave frequencies represent the color aspects of light (the colors in between the high-frequency waves of ultra-violet and the low-frequency waves of infra-red), which in turn represent emotions.

A solid relates to the world in a different way a liquid or gas does, while plasma dynamically interacts with the very substances of existence, energy (emotion) and magnetic fields (gravity or love). The strength of the magnetic field produced by plasma introduces a structure (math). Plasma is the physical manifestation of the phenomena of emotion. We are composed of matter (flesh and bone), liquid (blood and water), gas (the air we breathe) and plasma (the dynamic energies/emotions which produce our magnetic field and gravity) so we may relate with all of existence.

We are all composed of the four states of matter, but the chemistry in which we are put together slightly differs from one person to the next, causing dynamic changes in the way each person interacts with their environment. The dominant aspect of a person is related to the way he is assembled in relation to the four states of matter with an emphasis on his plasma characteristics.

People are born with a variety of dominant aspects because people are born within the spectrum of light, or the spectrum of emotion. The famous Swiss psychiatrist, Carl Jung, founded 12 archetypes which fit the personality types or dominant aspects of most people. For the purpose of framework, we will use some of these dominant aspects as examples to explain how the archetype or dominant aspect (aspect of light) an entity is reflecting is in direct correlation with the frequency (emotional perception) in which one relates with his or her environment.

For these examples, let's use: the artist, the explorer, and the hero. The artist, explorer, and hero each embody a wavelength of light which reflects their dominant aspect. This wavelength of light, whether it be blue, green, or orange is in direct correlation with the emotional perception (or frequency) in which each relates with his or her environment. For example, if all three archetypes fall in love, each of the dominant aspects will absorb, transform and emit their own emotional perception of love.

All types of people with all of their dominant aspects might experience falling in love, but in a slightly different way due to the influence of their archetype. The emotional experience of love is in direct correlation with the dominant aspect of a person. The dominant aspect of a person is the frequency (or wavelength of light) which will absorb the experience of falling in love and transform it into an emotional perception of love. Even though what is being experienced is the same (love), the way love is emitted will depend on the dominant aspect of the person experiencing love.

When two people fall in love, the way each one expresses love and receives the love of the other tends to be different and can more often than not be misunderstood or misinterpreted in some way. We all want to experience love, yet our emotional perception of love varies from slightly different to drastically different depending on our dominant aspect. This is all part of the puzzle of progress. It is through the emotional effort of understanding the language of love, transformed and emitted in different ways through a wide variety of archetypes (dominant aspects), that we are able to understand and experience love in all her wondrous hues.

Our dominant aspect sits at the core of our emotional blueprint, which doesn't change. People don't really change, they grow, evolve, and elevate. From the core of our emotional blueprint, from our dominant aspect, we expand. Sometimes we expand so far from the limited and confined person we once were that it may seem like we have completely changed into a different person. We've really just grown.

When we emotionally mature and expand wide enough, the way we absorb, transform and emit emotions will be grandiose in comparison to the narrow reflections of our emotions when we were emotionally immature. When we expand our emotional blueprint, our dominant aspect, we can then transform experiences, or emotion, or light, into more possibilities and emit a broader range of emotion. Expanding our emotional blueprint allows us to expand our own architecture of objective reality and experience.

Expanding the radius of light

A green plant represents the green aspect in the spectrum of light/emotion and thrives within a certain range or radius of light relative to the emotion of light it embodies.

The hue or color of emotion, also vibrates at a certain frequency. For example, the color of a flower emits a certain frequency which pulls/persuades and attracts what it so desires: the birds and bees.

Humans are each born into a dominant aspect of light, a unique emotional blueprint, yet we all have the potential and ability to embody and encompass the full spectrum, the entire range of existence through emotion. It is because we are not limited to the parameters of our design that we have the potential to attract anything we desire. This is the plight as well as the divinity of our design. As all other creatures are bound to the parameters of their aspect, humans are boundless and gifted with ability to expand or narrow their emotional blueprint through free will and choice.

We are the great heralds of structure and pandemonium. Within our emotional blueprint lives the potential and power to inflict inconceivable amounts of destruction and chaos, but also living within us is the potential and power to heal and mend all of creation through joy and love.

It is in the integration of our whole potential, the dominant aspect of light which we were born into as well as the ability to expand our aspect to encompass the full spectrum of light/ emotion, that we are able to discover our true purpose—the gift we were born to share with the world—so we may expand the experience of existence itself.

The Art of Existence

When an artist begins to arrange broad shapes of colors on a blank canvas, he or she is establishing the foundation for the mood or emotion of the piece. Once the foundation has been established, the artist builds on the colors and shapes to bring the piece to life through adding details.

The details require architecture (math) to create a structure which will hold the shapes and colors (emotion) within a design. Only when the broad shapes and colors have been successfully united within a grand design does the piece come together to reveal what everyone so greatly desires: a feeling.

A great artist masterfully composes an emotional medley, a grand connection and experience with whomever experiences his work. The observer and the art relate to one another through an objective experience. Art, like anything else, including reality, and existence itself, is a subjective experience between the observer and that which is being observed.

Reality is a unique emotional experience composed of relationships.

If one is blind, then light or color will translate into frequency, or sound. Music is also a representation of the spectrum of light. Emotion does not require sight to be experienced. Emotion can be translated through frequency.

If one is both blind and deaf, the spectrum of light and emotion will be interpreted through vibration, or feeling. Experiencing emotion through physical sensation is the most direct path to experiencing existence itself.

It is through sight, sound, and/or touch that one establishes the relationships necessary to experience the objective reality among all of creation. Taste and smell amplify the senses of sight, sound, and touch, intensifying the sensation and the emotional experience of the art of existence.

Heal the World

The emotional experience is why emotional intelligence and healthy boundaries are so important.

Emotional intelligence and healthy boundaries mediate our emotional experience as our emotional experience is responsible for helping us cultivate the reality we wish to project of the world.

Emotional intelligence and healthy boundaries are essential in cultivating balanced relationships with our loved ones, our environment, and most importantly, ourselves.

Understanding our emotions, as well as understanding that we have the ability to shift and transform them into something more productive, more creative, and more in tune with the harmony of energy all around us (the "flow" that so many Zen masters speak of), will allow us to project the peace, love, and joy which radiates within us out into the world.

Cultivating emotional intelligence and establishing healthy boundaries is what will ultimately heal the world, because by maintaining health in ourselves, we will maintain health in the world.

Role Play

Imagine this scenario:

You are young and you are as beautiful and vibrant as your ideologies and expectations in life. Perhaps you are even in love.

Think of how you feel in this scenario—how joyful and excited you are, and how the world holds such hope.

Then, you are suddenly confronted with opposition. Life begins to challenge your ideologies and proceeds to dismantle your expectations, one by one. Perhaps the person you love even betrays you in some way.

Think of how you feel in this scenario—how sad, angry, or depressed you may have become, and how dim the world seems and feels to you now.

Here's the fascinating part: the world hasn't changed, your emotions have. Your emotions have shifted, and thus, the world has transformed. All of your beautiful expectations and even your concept of love itself has turned. Your whole belief system has crashed, shaking and shifting the perspectives of what you deemed important. Naturally, you feel as though your emotions were flung from a catapult over the horizon of your healthy boundaries.

As your emotions hit the ground, exploding in an area so far from your comfort zone that you feel you will never be able to incorporate or integrate them within the parameters of your healthy boundaries again, you begin to despair. On top of being completely exposed and vulnerable, your emotions now lie outside the lines of your perceived limits like a shattered dream. Your once-beautiful and romantic fantasy transforms into a nightmare from which you don't know how to wake.

What a drama.

Our emotions shift our perspectives of the world.

Shifting Reality

Reality is influenced and distorted by the way we project our emotions. This is true for both the happiest and the saddest events in our lives.

When one falls "in love," reality shifts and becomes distorted in a highly euphoric way.

Just because one is experiencing and projecting a joyful disposition onto the world does not necessarily mean that their perspective is in any way more valid than one who is projecting sadness. Emotion shifts reality. One perspective of reality is as valid as the next because emotion in any form is an experience and expression of existence.

Now, to be truly happy (if there is such a thing), one must cultivate enough understanding, enough emotional accountability and maturity, that external circumstances are not so imperative to shift our emotions so drastically. If you truly wish to be happy, then be happy, no matter the circumstance.

True joy encompasses all energy—all vibration—all EMOTION.

The Joy of Progress

All this has been said before.

What no one seems to reveal, is how this is possible.

How do we embrace all emotion and keep certain situations or circumstances from triggering our emotions in such a way that our ability to experience joy and happiness isn't so easily influenced and affected?

Transformation

Before I begin to answer this question, ask yourself truthfully: Do you want to leave the comfort of your pain? Do you really want to transform or broaden your perspectives?

Growth is not easy, so answer this question honestly.

From what I have discovered, not everyone is actually ready to move on, and that is fine. Sometimes we must experience a stage in our cycle of elevation for prolonged periods of time before we are ready to move on.

If you are ready—truly ready—you will find this next topic extremely useful. It will serve as a method to free yourself from the stage you are stuck in so you may continue on your journey in the cycle of elevation.

If you are not ready, you may read the words and understand the messages, but remain stuck until you are emotionally ready to transform.

The Big Picture

In many cases, only partial messages regarding the attainment of one's purpose, divine connection, true happiness, and the mystery of existence have been conveyed. This is true in the case of most, if not all, organized religions or disciplines. The messages are scattered in bits and pieces throughout cultures. The messages have been mapped out in different ways among various spiritual practices and disciplines. This is what keeps the mystery of existence a secret.

In actuality, hidden knowledge, revelation of purpose, and divine meaning, aren't secrets. They are all accessible through the cultivation of karmic connections in the cycle of elevation

To discover meaning hidden in shadow, to reveal purpose behind the curtains of illusion you have to not only be willing to look, but unite the pieces of truth you discover into a dance, a symphony, a design which reveals the truth in all practices and disciplines, for the art of existence is painted into all versions of reality. You must look from a broader perspective. It is difficult to experience the exquisite beauty of a masterpiece if you are only focused on one aspect, or a tiny piece of the puzzle.

Every concept, teaching, religion, and practice is linked to another. The links which unite these disciplines can help explain and expand upon one another kind of like the internet. The internet helps connect us to what we want to know by offering us information related to our topic of interest. For example: Wikipedia, is knowledge linked to knowledge, linked to knowledge—a word, a term, a concept, can be expanded upon through the links imbedded within the information offered to us. If we stay within the parameters of one discipline then we take only the information provided to us without exploring the links which can expand our understanding.

Science can help explain existence, philosophy can help explain spirituality, math can be used to explain language and language can be used to explain math. Math provides the structure for existence while emotion (language) provides the content.

Geology—the rocks which provide structure and elements for soil and life—is just as essential as the water which rains from the sky, reshaping the terrain and giving life to the planet. Both geology and water are required to sustain the cycles of the Earth. Similarly, some practices may focus on prayer while others focus on gratitude, but we need to have a balance of both—we need to dream, to seek, to pray for attainment and understanding while acknowledging and having gratitude for the gifts we are showered with in order to be in alignment with the cycle of elevation. Additionally, our karma, or our sins need to be atoned for in order to elevate above the karmic cycle and reach nirvana, or to enter the gates of heaven. As people move toward a more holistic, multidisciplinary view, the humanity in all of us will be able to breathe a greater understanding of life.

Even the messages conveyed within this book are not complete. That's why everyone is urged to expand upon the messages in this book. Through direct revelation or an expanded view, we can experience these concepts in greater detail. A more complete experience will allow us to integrate a broader definition of any concept into our lives so we may expand human consciousness and experience every color of the rainbow as we sing, dance, and paint within the masterpiece of existence.

More than meets the Eye

You can't just look with your eyes. Relying on a sense which is limited only to that which we can see can lead to the omission or misinterpretation of truth, especially when the mystery hides in a shroud of darkness.

Some things we can't see—we have to feel. This feeling isn't shaped and developed by a belief, a hope, or even a desire. We do not create the feeling, we discover it—we reveal it. We connect with the feeling, for it is already there.

When we feel the true and authentic connection to the full spectrum—the dynamic emotional wonder and miracle within us— we experience the relationship we share with the wonders and miracles of the universe.

We need to unite all maps, all aspects, all light, and all versions of reality through authentic connection to discover what resonates as truth. When a mystery is revealed, it strikes an intuitive chord within ourselves, which in turn, exposes a direct relationship or connection with the mystery itself.

Partial messages and partial maps interpreted using only sight, or emotions heavily influenced by doctrines and beliefs, will keep us in partial understanding and can prevent the growth of our relationship with the mystery. We have to see that there is more to ourselves, to each other, to each piece of the mystery than meets the eye.

The Two

The concept of two describes the prevailing supposition that there are two halves or two sides to any situation or story: me and you, right and wrong, good and bad, Republican and Democrat, night and day, hot and cold—I could go on and on.

Though this idea of two is true, it is only a partial truth. The cycle of life, of existence, is much broader than the concept of two. I will expand on this later.

The One

Then there is the concept of one: only one way, one God, one purpose, one love, etc. Though this concept of one is also true, it is still only a partial truth.

How can the possibility for life, for the infinite potential of existence, manifest if there is only one way?

Again, we will come back to this later.

Framing the Question

You must understand that to find the answer to something elusive, you need to first ask the right question.

The next thing you must come to understand is that more often than not, even once you frame the question correctly, you will almost never be answered directly. Your question will often lead to more questions, for the mystery is as limitless as potential is infinite. Questions which perpetuate more questions is the reason why people find progress so puzzling. You may have noticed this book leaves some answers open to interpretation. Some questions are even left completely open. This book does not want to answer the hard questions about your life for you. You must be the one to do so through your creativity and logic. Only you will find the answers you seek. This book is simply a guide to help you align with the cycle of elevation so you may cultivate your inner voice and experience success in all aspects of your life, for yourself.

You may also have noticed that we have not directly answered the question asked in the above section titled, *The Joy of Progress*; how do we embrace all emotion and keep certain situations or circumstances from triggering our emotions in such a way that our ability to experience joy and happiness is less affected?

In keeping with the tradition of not answering any question directly, we will begin to answer this question by reviewing the previous stages in the cycle of elevation.

Chapter 12

The Puzzle of Joy

In chapter twelve we will focus our attention on the elusiveness of joy.

Everyone wants to be happy. For some, the quest for joy is comparable to a holy crusade. Many people believe happiness is something that will occur only after the achievement of an external coordinate, and thus, joy always seems to be just out of reach. The puzzle of progress seems to run parallel with the puzzle of joy, for there never seems to be enough of either to quench the thirst of humankind. Human beings tend to have an insatiable appetite for more. More progress, more joy. There is never enough of anything, and thus, progress and joy become overshadowed by a feeling of scarcity, a scarcity which threatens the joy and progress in our everyday lives.

It is the attention one devotes to his selfish desires which prevent him from understanding that progress is a universal phenomenon. Progress is always occurring, it is our demand to manipulate progress for our own personal benefit which prevents us from experiencing the ever turning and transformation of life as a wondrous, never-ending wheel of progress. The universe is continually progressing, and in turn, so are we.

Joy is a universal element of existence. Joy is something we would acknowledge as a universal constant if we weren't so busy trying to define joy within the parameters of our own selfish wants and desires. The puzzle of joy is that it doesn't dwell in any single element or aspect of life, but in all things, within every stage in the cycle of elevation. When we get caught up pursuing our own version of joy, that which we would manipulate joy to be, we shelter ourselves from the elements of joy which are constantly trying to shower us in its radiance.

Let's begin to understand the puzzle of joy with a dance of energies.

The Dance of Energies

To begin answering the question—how do we embrace all emotion and keep certain situations or circumstances from triggering our emotions in such a way that our ability to experience joy is less affected? I will call once again on the concept of the masculine and feminine energies, stage one and two in the cycle of elevation.

The masculine and feminine energies dance and swirl all around us. For review, masculine energy represents potential (the possibility of), while feminine energy represents formation, the transformation from potential into reality.

As human beings, we can get so caught up trying to discover and understand the balance between these two energies and the effort it takes to unite them in a harmonious way to achieve our dreams, that we forget that these are only but two energies.

The masculine and feminine energies are integral pieces in the formation of the universe, but are not the only aspects which compose the spectrum of existence. The cycle of elevation requires a circuit to be formed, and the masculine and feminine energies are not enough to complete the circuit.

There are more energies which need be discovered and integrated into our understanding so that we, as "conscious beings," can expand and progress in the cycle of elevation.

Dream Energy

Another form of energy (which we already went over) which is essential for the maturity of our emotions, is dream energy. Emotional maturity allows us to understand and integrate the limitless expression of emotion which dwells within us through the energy of dreams.

In stage three, dreams can act as either a destructive energy, a constructive energy, or any combination in between. Dream energy more often than not projects illusion and separation, the deconstruction or decomposition of what actually is. The other side of dream energy broadcasts unification, the connection between all things.

While feminine energy is responsible for the creation or formation stage of reality, dream energy is responsible for breaking down formation so it may be reassembled with a more relevant design. After the formation stage, dream energy is the next stage in the cycle of elevation (potential-formation-DREAM-hibernation).

Whatever is broken down, withers, or dies within the dream stage is not lost. Death isn't an end, just a stage in the cycle of elevation. Everything is "born again" but not necessarily in the same shape or form, for the potential for growth, for life, for existence, is infinitely evolving.

Mending and Weaving

Dream energy is not only needed to take things apart. Dream

energy is also needed to mend things or to bring them back together.

Creation and existence—those which are of the feminine aspect, Mother Nature herself—is lonely without a bond, a connection which unites all of existence together.

Our ability to relate to one another, to feel compassion, empathy, and most importantly, to acknowledge the divinity in another (or in anything for that matter) which reflects or mirrors the divinity within ourselves, springs from dream energy.

Dr. Martin Luther King Jr. even said it himself in his famous "I Have a Dream" speech, delivered on August 28, 1963:

> I have a dream that one day every valley shall be exalted, every hill and mountain shall be made low, the rough places will be made plain, and the crooked places will be made straight, and the glory of the Lord shall be revealed, and all flesh shall see it together.

Dream energy can separate or unite. We can divide ourselves up by race, or we can unite as one species. We can also cultivate any reality between or beyond those two aspects.

It is the reality between two aspects, two complements, which bring the possibility of anything to life.

What I believe Dr. King was suggesting in his famous, "I have a dream" speech is that one day every valley, those things which can be dark and mysterious shall be exalted, or come into light. The mountains of separation, the obstacles which are keeping us apart, will one day come undone or be made low through our will to unite. The hard and rough times we go through as a people divided will smooth out when we are able to come together. The detours of injustice we pursue on our journey to find truth will eventually lead us back to the path of justice, where the glory of love will be revealed, and the collective human consciousness shall experience it together.

Anything is possible if we come together and unite as a people, but we must unite with respect to the unique emotional blueprints of others. We must grow and expand our emotional blueprint with reverence for the potential of not just mankind, but the world.

When something brakes down, withers or dies, it is then united with the energies from which it was birthed.

When our bodies die, they go back to the earth to unite with the cycle of elevation, as a new enchantment, as potential waiting to be formed into something new.

Our spirits and all of creation must eventually unite with the flowing, cycling energies of joy and love (the emotional source of all energy) to continue on their journey to expand the possibility of elevation even further.

Dr. King's dream is an example of how individual links or cycles influence the elevation of the grand cycle. Dr. King's individual link, his dream, touched and influenced so many cycles that all the obstacles he spoke of were overcome by the combined effort of humanity (the collective human consciousness) working together.

The Debt of Want and Desire

Everyone wants what they want. Our divinity allows us to manifest any want into reality through enough willpower and effort. However, when a person's wants and desires are projected onto the unwilling backs of others, then no matter the achievement, there will never be a possibility for a shared experience of unconditional love and joy worth celebrating. Entire civilizations and empires have been built on the backs of slaves. Slaves who were stripped of their divine right to have and discover their own potential, to pursue their own dreams.

Manipulating and inhibiting the emotional blueprint of others to bolster and glorify the emotional blueprint of one's self creates an unfair and unbalanced monopoly in the spectrum of life. Instead of elevation (the expansion of the spectrum of existence), only an aspect of the spectrum of existence will be extended.

When a doctrine, crystallization, or belief structure overshadows the light, the frequency, the vibration, the beautiful hues and gifts of others, the scope of existence itself narrows as the spectrum of potential and possibility are extinguished, one aspect at a time.

When we begin to destroy the possibilities of existence, at some point, the price for life, the price to exist, can become too high a price to pay, for life becomes a debt rather than a gift of infinite possibilities which expand the experience of joy and love.

Emotional sabotage is a debt which needs to be paid and wiped clean. Emotions need to heal through balanced relationships before energies can realign with the cycle of elevation, so life may once again expand and extend to infinity and beyond.

Until this debt has been forgiven, love and joy will remain just out of reach, disguised behind a costume of artificial and material illusion—the desire for that which we want, rather than a relationship with what is.

Live and let live, or in a quote often attributed to Mahatma Gandhi, "May I live simply so that others may simply live."

Harmony

Everything seeks to find a balance in relation to the cycles of energy.

The cycles of energy, of the seasons, of life, of existence itself, are all intertwined and connected, like a web which is constantly breaking down and being added to. Some parts stay broken and some parts are mended, but new enchantments are always being woven in—as the cycle of elevation spins the web of existence in relation to the elements which influence it.

Elements of Influence

When we become unbalanced or stuck in one aspect, it affects not just our energies, but everything we come in contact with. Our sphere of influence becomes compromised.

A person's overall success is not measured by any single achievement, but the elevation of every aspect he is composed of with respect to balance. There are countless elements which make up a life, which must expand in order for a person to realize and experience the overall success and joy of life.

Impossible Questions

Even when a mystical book like the *I Ching*[2] is consulted, our questions are answered in the form of another question, which inquires how balance can be achieved in whatever problem we seek to solve.

When we look to discover our purpose and the meaning of life, the great masters ask impossible questions, like:

---

[2] The *I Ching* is an ancient Chinese divination text that interprets hexagrams formed by random methods to answer questions. The *I Ching* is attributed to Fu Hsi, a legendary emperor in China, who reigned approximately 5,000 years ago (though the exact date and author seem to remain a mystery); the book has changed over millennia as additions and interpretations have been added.

What would you do if you knew you could never fail?

What would you change in your life if money were not a factor?

When we ponder these questions, we tend to seek out concrete answers. We chase after an answer which will solve all of our problems, a be-all and end-all solution to the confusing chaos of life. What we forget to allow for are the changes that occur constantly and consistently throughout life. Life is constantly shifting, transforming from one energy to the next in a continuous cycle which is always evolving.

Absolute Answers produce Absolute Suffering

When we seek the attainment of anything without regard to the balance of energies which constitute the cycle of existence, we create our own suffering.

When we are in a state of suffering, the answers to the seemingly impossible questions (e.g., *what would you do if you knew you could never fail* or, *what would you change in your life if money were not a factor?)* will more often than not elude us.

Even if we discover an answer which may work for the moment, it is still ultimately inconsequential to attaining real joy because at some point or in some way, the be-all and end-all solution we adopt into our lives will prove to be not true or useful. When this happens, when this realization occurs, we may suffer all over again.

We cannot fall victim to outdated doctrines or cling to the nostalgia of how things used to be.

All things in Moderation

If we act with regard to harmony and balance, the path to joy appears almost magically. The seemingly impossible questions of purpose and meaning inquired by some "master" or "guru" pose as nothing more than a reminder of our intuitive genius. As Sherlock Holmes would say, "Elementary."

Our purpose, the meaning of life and of existence has already been attained. We have achieved it many times before. We have just forgotten.

Answering Impossible Questions

What would you do if you knew you could not fail?

The answer should be that you are already doing it. If you are not, then you should be actively pursuing a way to transition into doing it.

This will not be easy and there will be many instances where you feel you are failing, but you have to remember this is how dream energy works. To bring a dream into reality the dream must first be broken down. It will seem as though you are failing. From the broken pieces of your dream you must continue. You must allow your dream to be put back together and reconstructed in the proper way. You must allow the dream to reconstruct itself in the most relevant way— in the way it needs to. You must flow with the dream, almost as if you were in a dream sleep, for if you fight, your dream may turn into a nightmare. Connect with dream energy in a harmonious way and harness it to unite with your dream. Once your dream is reassembled, you and your dream will elevate with a fresh, new enchantment. This new enchantment and potential will weave relevance back into your dream.

There are no shortcuts in the cycle of elevation that I am aware of.

Move through the stages of the cycle of elevation with effort and respect and you shall not fail.

What would you change in your life if money were not a factor?

The answer should be nothing.

Why should money be such an influential aspect that you cannot be who you want to be or live the way you want to live?

Instead of living and working for money, perhaps more effort can be allocated into building healthy and strong relationships which produce assets. Put an emphasis on expanding your influence in service to others without selling yourself short. If you are able to do this with respect to harmony, money may cease to be an issue. Although the purpose of this book is not to detail the many ways you can free yourself of financial burdens while building financial assets, this is an important step to acquire more power (or time) and the freedom to share your unique gifts.

We have reviewed stage one, two, and three on our journey to reveal what true joy is. On to stage four.

Hibernation

Our journey in life is a part of the never-ending cycle of elevation.

Just as the human body gives rise to countless other cycles and systems in the body (beginning and ending with the cell), the cycle of elevation is the grand cycle which gives rise to infinite other cycles (beginning and ending with the atom), to which the foundation of life and all existence relates.

Potential, or masculine energy, manifests into reality through feminine energy, which is then processed by dream energy so it may be deconstructed and put back together in a manner which is more relevant to the ever expanding source from which it came. Dream energy brings us to the next stage in our cycle of energies: elevation.

Many people may not associate something like hibernation as a form of energy, but it is more than the slowing of metabolic processes. The caterpillar elevates through a stage like hibernation within its cocoon. When it is ready, the caterpillar emerges from its cocoon as a butterfly.

As a caterpillar emerges in its elevated form from its cocoon-encased hibernation, it begins the process of elevation all over again, although it now carries a higher purpose. The lower form of itself, the caterpillar, mechanically crawled around the earth consuming life. In its elevated form as a butterfly, it gracefully dances in the air helping to generate life as it propagates one of the most dazzling creations of all: the flower.

The butterfly will eventually die. The energy and physical parts of the butterfly will eventually reunite with the source of all creation. The source of all creation dwells within the elevation stage. Winter, hibernation, and night is where new enchantments are woven into the very fabric of existence. Potential expands within the elevation stage. The world and everything in it retains its magic and potency through the cycle of elevation.

So, how do we embrace all emotion and keep certain situations or circumstances from triggering our emotions in such a way that our ability to experience joy is less affected? Through elevation.

When the world is full of magic, no matter what situation or circumstance finds us, we are able to experience joy in all the enchantments of life.

Magic brings harmony to all emotions so we may experience unconditional   and   unaffected   joy.

Chapter 13

Four Seasons

Within chapter thirteen we celebrate the seasons—more-so the relationship between the four seasons and the four stages in the cycle of elevation. Chapter thirteen also brings relevance to the parts of the day; morning, noon, evening, and night and how these parts connect with the stages in the cycle of elevation. Relationships are everything, especially human relationships.

The Fantastic Four

In the stage of elevation, we come to rest in a balanced connection with all of existence. It is a place of magic.

From elevation we are primed to grow further. To do this we start the process or cycle of elevation all over again, beginning with acceptance.

Acceptance is potential—acceptance is potential because when we accept our responsibility for our actions, anything is possible, including the potential to understand.

Understanding is formation—the formation of potential into reality and the development of real knowledge from something we once did not know.

Integration is deconstruction and unification—the deconstruction of walls as well as the building of bridges between worlds and the unification of scattered realities into a multidimensional masterpiece.

Elevation is a place of magic—a place where new enchantments are woven into the very fabric of life, where all of existence expands within a harmonious slumber.

Spring, summer, fall and winter.

The four seasons are a hallmark to the four energies (potential, formation, dream, and hibernation) and the four principles of elevation (acceptance, understanding, integration, and elevation).

Celebrate

The four energies and the four stages of elevation are why we celebrate the seasons as well as other cycles, like the cycle of the moon. The four energies are also the reason we give reverence to the equinoxes. To be in tune with nature is to understand the cycle of existence and rejoice. When we embrace, celebrate, and give thanks to whatever cycle we are experiencing in relation to all of creation, we acknowledge our place in relation to all of existence.

The cycle of the four energies keeps us in balance and in good health. The energies speak to us in ways which nudge us through whatever stage is proving difficult to transition from.

Another Chance

When we become stuck, the cycles, the energies within us, fall out of harmony. Basically, our own emotions become stagnant and in desperate need of balancing. We need to move on to the next phase of our lives or we will begin to suffer. We suffer through the inability to evolve, elevate, and expand our potential.

When we are unable to move through the stages fluidly and

progress toward our potential, illness, fatigue, and depression begin to creep into our lives and take residence within our emotional blueprint. We begin to fall apart emotionally, mentally, and physically.

If we are unable to move on from what is blocking us, we may die.

Our physical bodies die in order to allow our souls another chance at elevation. The seasons and cycles continue whether we are ready or not, but we are always given another chance.

The Two Sides of the Dream Stage

Fall is one of my favorite stages in the cycle of elevation because this is where the most growth occurs.

When we are confronted with a challenge—whether it is physical, mental, or emotional—and we begin to integrate whatever we believe to be in conflict with us, we are entering into the dream stage in the cycle of elevation. The dream stage is where walls and limits, as well as aspects of ourselves which are proving to be untrue or not useful, are torn down and then put back together in a more relevant manner.

It has always been said that the veil between our world and the spirit world is at its thinnest during fall.

The celebration of Halloween may have evolved from the Celtic pagan religious festival of Samhain, where Celts burned bonfires and dressed in costume to ward off fairies who might cross over from the spirit realm. Celts believed that the border between our world and the spirit world could be breached during Samhain and would leave sacrifices, along with food offerings to appease monsters. The food offerings were also to benefit their ancestors who also might cross over as well.

Dia de Muertos is a Mexican holiday and another testament of the belief that the barrier between our world and the spirit world vanishes for a brief period of time in the fall so the physical and spirit world may interact.

The cycle of elevation states that fall is when walls are torn down and bridges are built to unite what we don't understand. The barrier between realms is breached in the fall to unite us with the spirit realm temporarily so we may expand our understanding of the mystery. These brief interactions with the spirit realm help human consciousness to grow and elevate.

Fall is the season associated with the beginning of the dream stage. It is not surprising that this season of uncertainty is often marked with depression and social crimes. The beginning of the dream stage is where we feel hopeless and powerless against the problems we are facing. We can feel like life has taken a turn for the worst and anything and everything we are confronted with can become too overwhelming to deal with. The beginning of the dream stage is fraught with mostly self-inflicted suffering. It may seem as if our world is breaking apart, and in a sense it is, but this is just the sensation of the irrelevant structures we have erected coming undone as we prepare to unite with the spirit realm. When we unite with the spirit realm successfully, a more authentic understanding can be integrated within us so we can create a more useful version of ourselves.

The tail end of the dream stage is where we bring back the knowledge from the spirit realm and put the scattered pieces of our reality back together to form a more relevant, multidimensional masterpiece which will help us move into the next stage in the cycle of elevation.

Many people get stuck in the dream stage. Perhaps that is why fall is fraught with so much worry and superstition. For if we get stuck in the dream stage (one can be stuck in any of the stages, not just the dream stage), we will be unable to elevate.

Illness and ignorance are associated with the dream stage, but so are healing and wisdom.

Sun-downing Syndrome

Have you ever admired a sunset? The way the cycle of energy integrates day into night is truly amazing. Sometimes it even seems as though you are witnessing a dream.

If we examine the common routine during the evening, the part of the day which is associated with the dream stage in the cycle of elevation (not night, which is the hibernation stage associated with elevation), we see a pattern, especially with kids and the elderly. These patterns have even been given a name: sun-downing syndrome. As the sun begins to fall, kids tend to become noticeably wilder while the elderly can become more anxious. This is all part of the cycle of energy in the integration or dream stage.

Evenings can be difficult as we anticipate entering a form of hibernation (sleep). With the end of the day rapidly approaching and sleep (or elevation) imminent, we can feel an intense pressure in the evening to break down the day in order to make sense of it all. We want to integrate everything we have experienced before turning in for the night so we can emerge from sleep as elevated individuals ready for the potential of yet another new and glorious day.

Though the morning is full of potential, sometimes it's hard to emerge from a night of hibernation or elevation. We tend not to feel fully-formed or activated until about midday. As the day progresses, we look forward to winding down and decompressing all that we endured in the evening.

The cycle continues.

The evening is a process of breaking down what we experienced throughout the day so we can re-assemble it in a way which allows us to move into the next day with new enchantments.

If we are able to break down and re-assemble our day properly, our reward is settling into a calm and peaceful night where we can weave the emotions we experienced into a more relevant understanding of our purpose in life.

Relevance

Mornings are just as spectacular as evenings. As the hibernation stage of night evaporates into light, a new potential is born—night elevates into morning as a new potential begins to materialize.

Anything in existence is only relevant for so long before it proves to be not true or useful. The necessity for consistent, fresh updates is why the cycle of energy transitions from potential, to form, to dream, to elevation, just to begin itself anew. Every day is a miniature cycle of the four seasons. Spring (morning), summer (midday), fall (evening), and winter (night). It is within the dream stage that form (life or manifestation) is broken down and put back in a way which allows it to expand, evolve, and elevate. From the rest-stage of elevation, the cycle of energy eventually moves again into potential so the new enchantments may be woven back into form.

By passing through the stages (spring, summer, fall, and winter) over and over again in the cycle of elevation, we become more and more familiar and adept with change and opposition. We grow in strength and fortitude while we expand our reach and influence into all the realms of which we are a part of. Like a tree who spreads its roots into the ground and extends its branches toward the heavens, we grow through the cycle of elevation and become more resilient, no matter what situation or circumstance may find us.

Relationships

The main reason relationships fail is because the people involved are unable to find a harmonious way to elevate together.

If one or more people in a relationship is stuck within a stage in the cycle of elevation, then the relationship may be unable to grow. The dream that would be, that could be, may fall apart. The relationship can break down into nothing more than a shattered dream. When a relationship is unable to elevate, it fails to stay relevant and the people involved can drift apart. The connection, the bond which held the relationship together can fade away. If you understand what stages in the cycle of elevation you and your beloved are having difficulty with, then you may be able to help one another move through these stages respectively until the both of you are once again re-aligned with the cycle of elevation in your own individual ways. Once you and your partner are re-aligned, your relationship may grow out of respect for one another's unique path in the cycle of elevation. You will grow together and you will grow as individuals.

Chapter 14

Soul Music

In chapter fourteen we explore the sound of existence. Sound (the vibrational frequencies of emotion), motion, and art are woven into the notes and melodies of the eternal symphony. Everything we do is a song which is added to the concert of existence. We are here to experience the music of life and expand upon it.

Energetic Vibrational Emotions

Everything is energy, which is vibration, which is ultimately emotion.

Emotion is constantly evolving and elevating through the cycle of elevation.

A rock is an expression of emotion. A tree is an expression of emotion. An animal is an expression of emotion. Each is vibrating at a certain frequency associated with its stage in the cycle of evolution and elevation.

The vibration of an object or living thing is determined by the energies necessary to compose and hold its form together in relation to the level and aspect of emotion it represents.

Earth is abundant with all manner of creation. All these varying levels and types of creation respectively represent an aspect of energy (vibrating in a certain frequency) which in turn represents an aspect of emotion. For example, inanimate states of matter (solids, liquids, gases, and plasma) and animate states of matter (plants, insects, animals, humans, etc.) are all different types of creation with varying aspects of energy. The vibrational energy of each is distinctive to the level of emotion an object or being represents in the cycle of elevation.

A rock vibrates at a certain frequency distinctive to the energy necessary to compose and hold it together. The rock's energetic vibrational frequency is relative to the level and aspect of emotion it represents in the cycle of elevation. A rock is form or expression of emotion, a tree is a form or expression of emotion, and you and I are a form and expression of emotion. The universe is composed of various expressions of emotion in every stage of evolution and elevation. The levels of dimension which the universe can conceive itself or be perceived is perpetually limitless through the emotional expansion of the cycle of elevation.

The OM of Emotion

Before our existence there was a humming—a sound so pure it sang through all of space breathing power (time) onto a canvas of limitless possibilities.

This vibration of sound energized the canvas (space) with dynamic melodies (algorithms), expanding the canvas into a multidimensional platform held together by the tune of love (gravity). The song continued to permeate this multidimensional platform filling every corner and crevice with power and emotion, creating a multiverse. The sound continues to reverberate through and beyond the known universe expanding every dimension with its divine gifts.

This song was and is the pure sound of existence: power (time), space (math/algorithms), love (gravity), and emotion (energy).

Tuned In

If you are tuned into music, if you are a musician in any way, think of where every sound, every note, every chord springs from within you.

All notes spring from emotion. Notes arranged in a structured sequence form the algorithms necessary to give dimension to the song, creating melodies and composing a distinct expression of emotion. A rock is an expression of emotion, a tree is an expression of emotion, a human being is an expression of emotion, and thus, so is a planet, a star, a solar system, a galaxy—the entire universe is made up of individual expressions of emotion which influence the expression of other emotions which are part of a cycle, which are part of a larger cycle, which are part of an even larger cycle, and so on and so forth creating a grand cycle which represents existence itself.

Everything we do is an expression extending from the source of energy responsible for breathing life into everything, the origin of existence itself: power (time), space (math/algorithms), love (gravity), and emotion (energy). Our actions are a way we can cast our melodies out into the multiverse so our song may be written into the musical concert of existence itself. Our hope is that we create a ballad which may enhance the emotional symphony of life in as many ways as possible.

When we are able to stay in the flow, when we are able to sing and dance with the cycle of elevation without resistance, the less we care to compare ourselves to others or measure ourselves against external coordinates. For the source of life resonates within us, helping to compose the notes with which we use to create our melody, so our song may sing to the tune of existence itself.

Expect Less, Accept More

The more we are able to accept, understand, and integrate where we are in the process of elevation, the less self-conscious we are about what other people think, and the more attention and reverence we give to the balancing and alignment of our emotions. With less attention on what others think, the more we are able to devote on balancing ourselves. When we are balanced we are better able to hear the music within our soul and transmit the sound of joy into everything and anything we do, no matter the circumstance.

Balancing our emotions and experiencing joy allows us to expect less and accept more.

An Unstoppable Force and an Immovable Object

When we get stuck in a stage of the cycle of elevation, the cycle cannot continue to flow and is unable to complete. When we get stuck in a stage of the cycle, whether it be potential, formation, dream, or elevation, we create a block in the flow of energy which serves as the basis for all of existence.

We can get stuck in any stage of the cycle of elevation, even the elevation stage. Sometimes to cope, people just want to stay at rest in the elevation stage, afraid to move on and acknowledge their potential, oblivious and aloof to the world around them.

Men tend to get stuck in the stage of potential (what could be, chasing dreams, and neglecting the feminine aspect which can achieve these dreams) while women tend to get stuck in the stage of formation (connecting and building relationships, more often than not with men who are caught up in their own potential and chasing dreams).

Whatever stage one finds himself unable to move on from, that stage begins to break apart and deteriorate into the dream stage. For example, if one gets stuck in the formation stage, obsessed with manifesting potential into reality, erecting monuments, and admiring what he has created, then he may get caught up in the reality of it all—the facts and data, the physical and superficial manifestations of life, chasing ideological concepts which reinforce the structure he bases his life on—then he will be prone and vulnerable to the other stages in the cycle of elevation which are constantly affecting him with change and growth.

If our structure is rooted in a foundation that is in opposition to change and growth, the flow of energy swirling all around us will eventually destroy our rigid structure, no matter how fortified it may be.

If we are stuck in any stage it will eventually fall apart into the dream stage where we will hopefully learn to reconstruct a more flexible—and thus more resilient—structure which can adapt to change and grow with the cycle of elevation.

If we do not reconstruct a more flexible and resilient structure, we succumb to the illusion that the rigid structure we have built is not cracking and falling apart all around us.

Denial.

The longer we remain in a stage in the cycle, the more prone we are to illness, disease, and life-threatening conditions.

So, what happens when an unstoppable force (the cycle of elevation) meets an immovable object (our rigid belief structure)?

We surrender to the source, the sound responsible for it all.

Death and Rebirth

When our energy shifts into the dream stage, even by natural means within the natural cycle of elevation, we enter a vulnerable period in our lives.

This is where everything we have taken in and formed into knowledge or understanding is taken apart.

The dream stage is where we are susceptible to illness, disease, and emotional conditions like depression.

The dream stage is where we are most exposed.

If we are unable to move the dream stage along to the other side of dream energy, where we are able to reconstruct our disassembled energy, we begin to deteriorate—figuratively and literally.

If we are unable to unite the potential and formation energies into something useful after they have been broken down within the dream stage, instead of moving onto the elevation stage of hibernation, our biological structure begins to break apart so our spirit can re-align with the cycle of elevation.

Death may occur from an accident, a crime, or by other means like old age, but we also play a role in the potential of our demise. If it must come to it, death is needed to release our soul from physical blocks so we may continue our journey.

This is all death is.

Death is not the end, but a way to merge with the source of energy—a melody which will allow us to flow back into the cycle—allowing our soul another chance at elevation.

Vulnerable Strength

If we wish to not die or fall victim to illness, disease, or depression, we need to find a way to allow our energy to continue to flow, evolve, and elevate.

The extremes we experience in life are challenging, but these extremes also allow us to integrate a broader understanding of life.

When we experience extremes, we become vulnerable and come to a crossroads. Fight or flight. One path leads to elevation, and the other to destruction, and it's not always the same path.

All paths eventually lead to death and re-birth in one way or another, but the manner of which the music of our soul is absorbed by the symphony of existence is ours to choose.

Expanding our Sphere of Influence: Comfort, Limits and Boundaries

Our understanding of life, of existence, is relative to what we have experienced. What we know and what we are comfortable with expands as we mature. As we are exposed to a broader variety of experiences, our boundaries, our limits, and our understanding widens.

The extremes we contend with as we age are pushed and extended to places further than we ever thought possible. What we were once uncomfortable with, what we once believed was impossible, can sometimes become natural.

Here is an example of how we can reveal our potential, expand our boundaries, and elevate:

When I was a kid, riding a bike was terrifying and at times seemed impossible. I kept at it, though, and continued to push myself until riding a bike transformed from the impossible to the possible. With even more practice and dedication, riding a bike expanded even further from possible to second nature. Eventually, riding a bike felt like an extension of myself.

We need to experience and embrace all sorts of extremes (with emotional intelligence and within healthy boundaries), pushing our limits in a variety of aspects, so we can integrate all the forms of energy (emotion) which move us through the cycle of elevation, over and over again.

Whatever we pursue and experience eventually becomes a part of the music of our soul.

The Six Million Dollar Question

Here's a great question: Why is elevation so important? Why should anyone be so concerned with elevating, especially if there is no end or peak we can summit?

The answer is simple: Elevation is important so that we may continue to expand our experience of joy into all aspects of existence. By expanding our experience of joy into all aspects of existence, we can connect with joy no matter the circumstance.

When we get stuck, we only experience a narrow perspective of joy which leaves us feeling frustrated, disconnected, lonely, and depressed (yes, depression is a form of joy, remember, as discussed in chapter 11, all forms of emotion, even suffering, is an extension of joy). We become prisoners within our own self-inflicted misery.

To move on from depression, loneliness, or any other emotion, we must continue to elevate.

If we do not move on, we fall ill. If we cannot find a way to allow the energy (our emotions) to continue to flow, we will deteriorate and may eventually die.

Whether or not we find a way to continue to elevate in life, when we die, our emotions, our sound, our song—our soul music—will continue on the journey in the cycle of elevation.

Music is Life

Even musical genres which identify with lower vibrational emotions, like the blues, spring from the core of the spectrum of emotion: joy.

We connect through music so well because music is the vibrational medium to which we can relate our own frequency. In turn, the frequency or vibration we are experiencing at any moment is identified as a certain type of emotion. For example, if we are depressed then perhaps the blues sing to our souls. If we are happy and full of excitement then perhaps pop music is the genre we connect with. Whatever type of music we relate with at any given moment represents an aspect, a variation of sound, which springs from the core of vibration within us: joy.

Ever since the cultivation of sound into song, music has evolved and elevated. What was once cutting-edge sound for one generation is outdated and irrelevant music to the next generation.

Music evolves and elevates so quickly and dramatically, branching off into so many genres, because emotion is constantly expanding, evolving, and elevating through the cycle of elevation.

Chapter 15

Inner Voice

Chapter fifteen illustrates just how important our inner voice is when it comes to the development of our emotional maturity. The manner in which our inner voice responds when faced with a challenging situation (or any situation for that matter), will heavily impact and influence our behavior and actions. Our ability to lead and to heal, not just others, but more importantly ourselves, dwells within the emotional maturity of our inner voice.

Discipline

Why is it important to understand that emotion is the force behind both energy and the first language? It's important to understand emotion as both energy and language so we may learn to communicate effectively and clearly, as well as identify needs. Once basic needs which are low in the hierarchy of needs are met, a person can operate at a higher frequency in terms of energy. Emotion helps communicate needs in the most effective way possible (like a baby crying or body-language in a non-verbal adult) so needs can be met allowing energy (emotion) to elevate or mature.

Satisfying needs through effective communication can eventually lead to emotional maturity—if one also learns to be disciplined.

Emotional maturity helps a person continue to flow in the cycle of elevation. When we are free from blocks we can operate from a state of balance.

Our potential is most accessible when we are in harmony. Harmony is a state sustained by symbiotic relationships that begin within ourselves and extend out into our environment. To achieve harmony, one must have discipline. So, to reach our potential, one must be disciplined.

Discipline is repetition within structure. Nature is a repetitive flow of energy within the structure (or cycle) of elevation. The seasons, the cycles of the moon, the rising and setting of the sun etc., are all testaments to this.

Nature is disciplined, yet we can never predict her. She can be gentle, warm and bright one moment, and harsh, cold, and dark the next.

Nature flows freely with the cycle of elevation because nature is composed of symbiotic relationships that naturally operate without any blocks. Nature does not regret or dwell, anticipate or predict, but is always moving, adapting, and responding (flowing) in the moment. Nature encompasses all extremes and is continuously shifting her alignment to be in sync with the cycle of elevation.

Nature may be operating within a structure—however, the structure is pliable enough to promote new possibilities yet strong enough to hold everything together.

This balance of flexibility and strength produces the ability to expand and change—to evolve and elevate.

We may aspire to cultivate our inner voice to the tune of Nature.

Leader, Alpha, Healer

If a person is out of balance and is unable to communicate his or her needs clearly and effectively, a block is formed, taking him or her out of the flow, out of alignment with the cycle of elevation.

When two or more people are trying to work together, and both or all of them are out of balance and unable to communicate effectively, it will almost always be impossible for them to achieve some sense of discipline and harmony together. Harmony must be attained so people may access their potential and fulfill the requirements necessary to elevate, individually and collectively.

Without a leader, alpha, or healer to help guide the team back into the flow and into a balanced state, communication will remain broken and the needs of the people involved won't be met. Unfulfilled needs keep the team operating at a low emotional frequency, near the lowest levels of the hierarchy of needs. The frequency of the lower levels is a wavelength of scarcity and uncertainty.

The leader, alpha, or healer is both burdened and honored with the authority and responsibility to lift a person or group up and out of discord, and elevate the individual or group to a state of harmony. Once needs are met and harmony is achieved, the team can operate closer to its full potential.

A leader, alpha, or healer can only ask the team to be as balanced as he or she is, for a team can only aspire to rise to the level of their leader.

If we wish to be leaders or healers, we will only be as potent or effective as we are balanced. We cannot ask others to follow our rules, boundaries, and limitations if we ourselves are not disciplined enough to establish, implement, and apply our own healthy boundaries. Basically, we must lead by example. We cannot ask others to do as we say and not as we do.

I cannot ask or expect someone else to be calm if I myself am unable to remain calm.

Joy, love, and affection can only be properly conveyed, received, and experienced if the parties involved seek to be in alignment with one another.

Our inner voice is our leader, our alpha, and our healer. We must cultivate a symbiotic relationship with our inner voice if we wish to elevate toward our purpose in a harmonious way.

Maturity

Another responsibility of a leader, alpha, and healer is to provide protection and guidance. Before we come into emotional maturity, we look to others to protect and guide us. We need support from a leader to show us a viable path toward maturity.

As we transition into maturity, we must come into our own potential and become our own leader, alpha, and healer. This is why cultivating our inner voice is so important.

We mature through our emotions.

Emotions are our first language and the language in which we interact and communicate with ourselves and the world. Though we are all connected and require support from countless cycles to sustain our existence, we need to be emotionally resilient, we need to be emotionally mature enough so we can be as resourceful as possible to at least support ourselves. We can come to support ourselves by applying our understanding of the cycles.

With the proper guidance we can cultivate the emotional maturity and endurance necessary to become our own leader, alpha, and healer.

If we elevate even further, we can guide others to cultivate their inner-voice so they may find their own path as a leader, alpha and healer.

Guide

People mimic or mirror the emotions or vibrations of others, but are always drawn toward balance.

If we wish to inspire and promote elevation through helping others overcome emotional blocks, then we must guide them toward balance by being balanced ourselves. We need to light a path through example by being a calm yet assertive guide.

Our inner voice is our original guide. It is the most authentic and truthful sound we will ever hear. It penetrates every emotion and influences and orchestrates every decision and action. Our inner voice is the guide which governs how we process and act in response to our circumstances and surroundings.

A good leader, alpha, or healer will remain as balanced as possible, no matter the circumstance, no matter what strain the environment places on him or her. A powerful leader, alpha or healer strives to cultivate symbiotic relationships, for harmonious relationships produce clarity in consciousness, the key element in decision-making and critical thinking.

Harmony promotes clear and effective communication.

A calm, assertive, and harmonious inner voice will literally lead an individual to success and inspire others to follow.

Chapter 16

Re-Enchantment

In chapter sixteen we will become re-enchanted with the concept of the "One" and the concept of the "Two" in a way which will bridge and expand the concepts of both. We will then visit how extreme ideologies in any doctrine of belief can lead to the severing of one's soul.

The One, Revisited

So, back to the concept of the Two and the concept of the One.

The concept of the One is only a partial truth because the one is composed of infinite aspects. Whatever the One is to you, (for it doesn't have to be represented by joy) I think we would agree that the One encompasses all.

The One is all that is and all that isn't.

The One is the possibility of something and the possibility of nothing at the same time.

Whatever we associate the One with, it is only a partial truth, for we cannot define the One through any meaning or definition.

If we experience some euphoric emotion or some feeling closely associated with true love, we might come to say something like, "Yes! This is it—this is the One! This is God—this is joy!" Yet, if this feeling or euphoric experience is defined by finite parameters in any way, if it does not encompass all possibilities including the possibility of nothing, then it is only a partial aspect of the One.

The One is everywhere and aspects of the One are within everything.

We can experience different versions and variations of the One wherever we are, whenever we want, as long as we are open and willing to identify any and all aspects as only a portion of the totality that is the One.

Absolute solutions eventually prove to be not true or useful, and thus, elusive because the One is constantly shifting, expanding, and evolving in relation to the cycle of elevation.

There is no one way to the One because all ways ultimately lead to the One.

When we limit ourselves to only one path, we limit our experience and understanding of the One.

Limiting our experience and understanding ultimately creates unhealthy boundaries that become too rigid (the gospel truth, crystallized doctrines), and thus, susceptible to the unstoppable force of growth and change which are essential elements in the cycle of elevation. A structure which is too rigid will eventually crack and break under the weight and influence of growth and change, pulling the structure toward the deconstruction phase of the dream stage. When foundations are torn apart, the duality of clinging to old ways and/or embracing new possibilities can begin the process of promoting the idea of the Two.

The Two, Revisited

If we embrace the deconstruction state of the dream stage

without regard and respect to balance, then we can succumb to the ideology of you vs. me.

When we are faced with opposition, we can become neurotic. This neuroticism is used to defend the identity and doctrines which in actuality are very sensitive and utterly irrelevant aspects when compared to the living cycles which compose the beauty of existence itself.

The defense of a righteous ideology can lead to the manifestation of war, a war between what you hold to be "the only way" to the One and anyone or anything which seems to oppose or contradict it.

This war is actually brandished upon all aspects of the One which fall outside the imaginary lines of your ideology. The One is cleaved in half so the two fragments can be misidentified and manipulated with false labels like; right and wrong, good and evil, night and day, and so on and so forth, so that you may righteously justify your path as being above all others.

As we separate ourselves from all other possibilities to defend a sole aspect which we believe to be "the only way" to the One, we ourselves become irrelevant, for we have removed ourselves from the infinite spectrum of existence, the ever-changing and evolving cycle of elevation. Therefore, that which we are trying to protect and promote has thus become isolated from the miracle and mystery of life. We defend a sensitive and irrelevant aspect which only lives because of our desire for it.

Something which has been removed from the relativity of existence immediately dies.

Doctrines and crystallizations are essentially aspects which have become severed from the connection to the One and cycle of elevation. These detached expressions eventually become inapplicable and irrelevant to the infinite potential of the One.

Severed Soul

Going to the extreme of defending your ideologies can lead to genocidal tendencies. This happens when one loses his soul in pursuit of building an artificial world completely separate from the source of life/creation/existence.

The greatest example I can think of is Hitler.

When you separate a petal from a flower, the petal wilts and dies. When you sever the vital connection between an aspect and that which gives it life, meaning, and purpose—it becomes corrupt, perverse in purpose, and in many ways, destructive.

An aspect isolated from its source of energy, or emotion, falls away from the cycle of elevation, and therefore—instantly becomes irrelevant. It immediately begins to be broken apart by the dream stage so the aspect can once again unite with the source of all energy and continue on its journey in the cycle of elevation.

Hitler's movement, his Reich, was conceived from a very narrow and extreme perspective of the One.

He masterfully manipulated his crystallized doctrine, his severed aspect, to appeal to a person's lowest emotional frequency. He seduced people with a promise of grandeur, a greatness which could be righteously achieved if they just threw all reason, all respect for balance and discipline out the window, and allowed their inner voice to remain immature, impulsive, and extreme in nature. A shortcut which many believed in and embraced, but as I noted previously—there are no shortcuts.

Extreme aspects elicit and trigger impulsive emotions which are so low in frequency that they drown out all sense and sensibility. These low frequency emotions can arouse a dangerous passion in people—romantic illusions which can lead to delusions of grandeur and superiority.

Hitler was able to gain support and momentum in his campaign of terror in a perverse way which was completely severed from life, existence, and the cycle of elevation.

The thing is, people do this all the time, just on a much smaller scale, and mostly to themselves. It's part of their self-inflicted suffering.

This is why there are healers who specialize in an art called soul retrieval.

What you have to remember is that everyone is a healer. All a real healer does is guide one who has forgotten who they are, to the healer within themselves.

Ultimately the most effective healer is yourself.

Stage 5: The Cycle Continues

A new beginning. Stage five is really just a continuation of the cycle of elevation. From elevation (winter) a new potential (spring) is born. With each spring comes new enchantments—updates and upgrades woven into the possibility of what might be.

Chapter 17

Updates and Upgrades

Chapter seventeen is full of amazing theories and possibilities. The natural cycle of elevation, which is responsible for creating an elevated level of consciousness (human beings), may have inadvertently spawned an alternate and artificial cycle created by the very conscious beings the natural cycle produced, to elevate and expand consciousness even further. It all begins with zeros and ones, and ends with your own path toward unlimited potential.

Until next time, farewell.

Light and love on your journey.

Zeros and Ones

The possibility of something: potential = zero.

Potential is represented as zero because potential is formless. Though potential is limitless, it takes no form.

The creation of something: formation = one.

Formation is represented as one because the formation or manifestation of anything is just a variation, an aspect of the One.

Zeros and ones arranged in various sequences and combinations create the universe and everything in it.

The Artificial Cycle

Even a computer system is subject to the cycle of elevation.

First there is an idea of what can be, a program that will help amplify human ability and potential in some way. Next, there is the creation and formation of the software and hardware.

The first version of the program tends to be full of holes which are vulnerable to cyber-attacks. The glitches and cyber-attacks break down the program to expose as many weaknesses as possible.

The program is then redesigned and reengineered in a more relevant way. The program is elevated or upgraded to a newer and better version—program 2.0, so to say, where the process begins all over again.

Consciousness 2.0

Even the source of the code is in sync with the cycle of elevation: zeros and ones.

Though people are responsible for typing in the code, these people are motivated by emotion to create not just the program, but the whole operating system itself.

Emotion is still the source of all creation and energy, even when it comes to artificial intelligence.

All that needs to happen for humans to create a new form or version of consciousness is to unite artificial intelligence with emotion.

The language of the universe is very much like the code of a computer program or operating system.

The missing piece which will transform all the advancements in technology and artificial intelligence into real intelligence, or consciousness, is emotion.

The scientists who cracked the code of DNA were baffled by how much "extra" space they seemed to find in DNA. The information which is necessary to create a biological structure doesn't seem to need all the "empty" space within DNA. There is so much unknown data which seems to be represented as blank, unnecessary code, or empty space in DNA which scientists can't seem to explain. Why does DNA have all this "junk" space?

What if all this "junk" space is necessary to expand and elevate to our full potential? Or, what if all the "junk" space in our DNA is actually our emotional blueprint? The dominant aspect of our character which gives a person his or her unique perspective, and through evolution, expands and evolves with the cycle of elevation… Wouldn't that be interesting?

Everything is Emotion

All over the world, people speculate and debate the origin and meaning of consciousness.

Where does it come from? What is it? Why is it?

The general consensus of all the informational theory which is written about consciousness is that it comes from the mind. From everything that I have heard and read, it is because of the evolutionary and revolutionary human mind that consciousness was born.

Why then is it that artificial intelligence, as advanced as it is, is still so far from mirroring consciousness?

We model technology from the biostructure of the mind,

believing that if we are able to develop a breakthrough algorithm which parallels the magnificence of the human brain, that perhaps then we will be able to inject consciousness into a mechanical, man-made machine.

The question I ask is, what good is intelligence without a connection, a relationship with existence? What about emotions? Also, if we are to play god and grant emotional intelligence (consciousness) to an artificial being of our creation, is it also necessary with regard to ethics and out of respect for balance to give such a being emotional freedom?

Or, do we just desire unconscious yet intelligent, emotionally void slaves?

If we dive deeper and look within, to the root of where the brain receives direction, from where it receives the messages needed to maintain all the processes of the body, we discover what motivates the brain to not only run the autonomic nervous system and direct metabolic processes, but command the body to act and react the way it does in pursuit of both physical pleasure and abstract desire: emotion.

The Space Between

So far, if you haven't given up on this book and have kept a very open mind, we have established that everything is emotion. Everything has an emotional blueprint—not just animate conscious beings, but inanimate physical objects as well.

If joy illuminates all of existence with light, and love weaves through all creation, connecting and holding all of existence together through gravity, then what about the spaces between the manifestation of emotion—the platform or field in which the physical manifestations of emotion operate?

What is space?

The space between all emotions is math.

Everything has a complement. Everything desires something and is desired by something. Everything seeks a symbiotic relationship.

Emotion is to math as the flower is to the bee.

The field, platform, or space in which emotion is able to operate and travel is math. Dynamic, fluid, evolving, flowing algorithms which create the structures and paths for emotion to expand, evolve, and elevate.

Math is the other half, the other side of emotion. Without math, emotion would have no means of order, no structure in which to be expressed in a comprehensible way.

Emotion is disorganized and chaotic.

Without the proportionate algorithms which help stabilize emotion through a structure (a structure which is both adaptable and in alignment with the cycle of elevation), existence would be something completely different. Perhaps it wouldn't be existence at all. Perhaps it would be pandemonium or chaos, or worse: an empty abyss or void.

Just as life started out simple on planet Earth, math started out simple in the universe.

As joy and love expanded to create different families of life and existence, math expanded into different branches, producing more and more complex algorithms to support an ever-evolving existence for emotion to occupy.

Space is like an architectural blueprint. Architects and engineers use math to create a blueprint on a blank field of paper to map out a theoretical structure.

Once the blueprint is completed, the structure starts to come to life in real time and space through the use of applying the theoretical algorithms on paper and manifesting it into reality.

Nature does this as well through the golden rule and sacred geometry. Nature is the greatest architect and engineer that ever was.

Blueprints and math. Math and blueprints. This combination is how all great monuments and wonders are made.

Some monuments are flesh and blood. Some wonders are endowed with more than just emotion, but the miracle of consciousness.

You and I are composed of a matrix of math which house wondrous emotions full of potential.

The emotion we house within our divine structure is so advanced, so evolved and elevated, that our software (Our emotional core) must be constantly upgraded as we mature.

From early childhood all the way into our adulthood we learn about language, pain, art, love, math, anger, ethics, excitement, social skills, etc. Our software, our emotional core (living within our gut) must be continuously upgraded before we are capable of becoming full-fledged and self-sufficient members of human society.

The design of our brain, when it was conceived, gave birth to a new branch of math. A branch of math composed of algorithms that seem to defy possibility.

Needless to say, these algorithms have not yet been discovered, even with the advent of quantum supremacy in computing.

These algorithms are not finite, but infinite and dynamic, helping to create the very structure of our reality.

The architecture of the human mind has united with the energy of human emotion to produce a miracle: consciousness.

Consciousness is a byproduct of the cycle of elevation.

To be in alignment with the grand cycle, every algorithm is persuaded to produce structures to hold or carry emotion through the cycle of elevation. As emotions evolve to expand potential, so do the algorithms.

There are limits to our hardware. The biostructure of our brain can only handle so many rotations and upgrades in the emotional cycle of elevation. Sort of like how the heart can only beat so many times before it conks out.

No matter what stage of elevation we are in when we conk out, we strive to progress toward our prime.

Reaching the pinnacle of our design within a lifetime is the definition of our prime and is a little different for everyone. Each of us is capable of reaching our prime, but whether we do or not is mostly up to us. I say mostly because sometimes other factors (of an extreme nature that are out of our control) affect our ability to move toward our prime. Sometimes we pass on pre-maturely. Sometimes external energies can oppress our ability to achieve our prime. Whether our inability to reach our prime was due to our actions, an accident, or the actions of another, the cycle of elevation always allows us another chance to elevate in one way or another.

If or when we reach our prime, we push the limits of what is possible, and thus, expand the possibility of existence which in turn raises the bar for the next generation. The next generation will hopefully be inspired and push the possibility of existence even further.

If or when we reach our prime depends on our emotional maturity.

The physical structure of our bodies has an algorithmic duration which is in tune with the cycle of elevation. Remember every structure, every creation must eventually move into the dream stage where manifestation (including our perception of reality) is broken down so it may be reassembled in a new and more relevant way. The more we can evolve and elevate emotionally during our timeline, the more the algorithms can evolve and elevate to reach their prime, updating the divine architecture which is physically responsible for carrying our emotions forward in the cycle of elevation.

Algorithmic structural durations are why nothing lasts forever.

There is no hardware, no algorithmic structure with an infinite duration which can accommodate the continual elevation of the perpetually expanding emotional software it carries indefinitely.

Evolution produces new structural designs (biostructures) to house elevated software (emotions).

The inability for a physical structure to permanently hold an expanding emotional core also accounts for why there are no absolute answers or fixed positions in quantum physics, the universe, or existence for that matter.

As our emotions expand and become more complex, so in turn do the algorithms which hold them. It is similar to how the software advancements of a computer give rise to hardware advancements (micro-chips and nano-technology).

Everything must run its course, whether it comes into its prime or not, in respect to the cycle of elevation.

Potential isn't about perfection, but progression.

You, I, and even the seemingly blank spaces between everything around us in the universe (which are far beyond our comprehension), are composed of a matrix of math, structures which house emotion in various stages of the cycle of elevation.

This matrix is in tune and alignment with the grand cycle of elevation. The sound, the song, the music which gave birth to it all: joy.

Upgrade

The biostructure of the human brain is evolution's version of a hardware update. No matter how advanced the hardware is, a software update is necessary to maximize and push the limit of a structure's capability.

Emotion is elevation's version of a software update.

The miracle of emotion is that it can be updated as we grow.

As one ages and transitions in life from toddler, to child, to adolescent, to adult, our emotional software has the ability to update as we grow.

The version our software (emotional maturity) is able to update to is contingent upon our own emotional intelligence and the healthy boundaries we have cultivated and established. For we will only mature if we learn how to master our emotions. Mastering our emotions will allow us to establish the kind of boundaries which will protect us while remaining flexible enough to keep expanding our potential. As we expand, mature, and grow we will build the bridges and harmonious relationships necessary to experience what we truly desire: authentic connections. All this this takes discipline. All this takes harmony. All this takes a massive amount of joy.

Though we need others to help guide our emotional maturity at first, to help form and develop our emotional software to a functional version in the early developmental stages of our life, we are ultimately charged with advancing our own emotional blueprint. The architectural algorithms of our own human potential and consciousness will begin to bloom once we conclude our rite of passage.

A guide is necessary but not responsible for achieving the

potential we are capable of. We ourselves are responsible for reaching the pinnacle or prime of our design within our lifetime. A knowledgeable and experienced guide in our formative years is highly beneficial, but not a determining pre-requisite for the evolution and elevation of our existence. Where the teachings of our guide may fall short—the world will find a way to fill in the gaps of our education.

From a functional emotional platform, we are not only able to experience an emotional connection with our environment, but we are also able to interact with the world in a way which allows us to express our emotions in an artistic and creative way.

Our pursuit of creative expression and emotional connections should be practiced with respect to the needs and obligations of life. For efficiency purposes, we develop habits to navigate the needs and obligations of life to ensure we the have the time to pursue our creative passions.

Habits help us stay true to our responsibilities, but must be periodically broken to release the spontaneity necessary for us to share our unique aspect with the world through the authentic and unhindered expression of our emotions.

Habits

It is through our habits that our lives start to develop an emotional pattern which runs in the background of our lives, like the autonomic nervous system of our body, or the operating system of a computer.

If we don't monitor our habits and consciously change them from time to time, then our actions and reactions to certain stimuli and situations become predictable and robotic.

Though habits are generally beneficial to us, we must be careful of our habits because our habits create an emotional cycle. This emotional cycle can eventually become embedded into our emotional blueprint like coded software. Basically, what I am saying is that it's easier to learn than to unlearn. When our habits, our emotional cycle becomes embedded into our emotional blueprint, it can be difficult to expand and grow. Our ability to adapt becomes compromised because many of our habits, the emotional cycle we have embedded into our emotional blueprint can be difficult to overwrite and unlearn. One of the hardest things to do is give up or change a predictable system which we count on to manage our lives. Navigating life can be full of uncertainty and just plain overwhelming if we don't have a stable and predictable system in which to operate. Though, there must be a balance. Life can also prove to be just as difficult to navigate within the confines of a closed system which is outdated and irrelevant.

Through predictable systems we may find a way to interact with the world without disrupting and challenging the emotional sensitivity we experience when we engage with our environment, but this method doesn't account for the one constant in life: change.

Ultimately, we may be alive, but without resiliency, without progress, and above all, without adaptation, we are just experiencing life as an outdated computer system in desperate need for an upgrade to our emotional operating system.

As humans with elevated consciousness, we need to cultivate emotional intelligence and establish healthy boundaries to minimize threats in our life, similar to how a computer employs virus protection to keep it from crashing.

Virus protection helps identify danger in a similar way to how healthy boundaries should, by containing or blocking potential threats, yet still allowing essential information to get through. We need to be able to integrate outside information safely so the necessary upgrades can be installed into our emotional software.

Upgrades expand the capabilities of our emotional core allowing our system to continue to perform at its optimal potential.

Accept what is useful, understand and disregard what is not, and integrate or add what is essentially your own.

You are your own version of reality.

When you are able to accept, understand, and integrate who you are with a certain level of grace, a certain level of balance, then you will upgrade or elevate your system, your consciousness.

Enlightenment.

Emotional Perspective

You must not be afraid to add what is essentially your own.

Through our creativity we construct theories, we even invent and project fantastic stories about what we don't understand so we can venture forth into the unknown from a safe and secure place (this book for example). From our fortress of solitude, our island of resilience, we try to find the missing pieces of whatever puzzle we are trying to put together.

Sometimes to better understand the puzzle we need the perspective of another (who comes from a completely different reality) to help expand our vision and boundaries. Sometimes we need to see something in a different light so we can figure out how it all fits together.

The more minds, the more worlds, the more versions of reality that are bridged together to form an interconnected web of existence, the more complete and clear the spectrum of existence becomes.

We all have a piece of the puzzle to share in the mystery of life, love, and the ultimate experience of existence in the universe.

241

The Journey

One does not learn and incorporate all this knowledge and wisdom from a book.

Your emotional blueprint is not cataloged and filed somewhere within the pages of some magic tome or divine manual.

You come to understand your emotional blueprint through experience.

You must learn through doing, and make many mistakes in the process.

Though there are many schools and teachers devoted to the enlightenment of human consciousness, a person's journey toward elevation and emotional balance is very personal.

No matter what you discover in books, learn in school or are taught by some great and wise old master, it is ultimately up to you to apply the lessons you deem appropriate for your own personal journey.

Just remember that on your path to emotional elevation and enlightenment, the things you want to happen will very rarely go the way you expect them to, and the things you tend to avoid are usually what you need to confront and integrate so you may move forward.

Also, never forget that the world will teach you more than any book, any school or any master, if you are aware and disciplined enough to let it.

The Four Guides

All this has been revealed to me through multiple platforms, but the majority of the messages that have been conveyed come from four main sources:

▫ A Shaman I have not physically met, yet guides me through spirit quests.

▫ The area in and around our equator, where Mother Nature displays her genius, creative potential. Where feminine energy supports and connects us all.

▫ The cosmos and the heavens.

—and of course—

▫ The aspect within myself which mirrors it all.

Afterword

If you wish to continue learning, please visit my website: LuluBabaBooks.com and sign up for my mailing list. I will only send out announcements of new books, programs and workshops.

Also, if you have any questions pertaining to the contents of this book and how you can apply the principals and concepts mentioned to help you achieve balance and success, feel free to reach out in an e-mail with any questions. I will be more than happy to help you any way I can.

More from the Author

www.LuluBabaBooks.com

Discover more stories that promote a higher level of inner awareness through asking questions and self-reflection.

Each story teaches: acceptance, understanding and integration, so children may learn to celebrate in all the differences of the world.

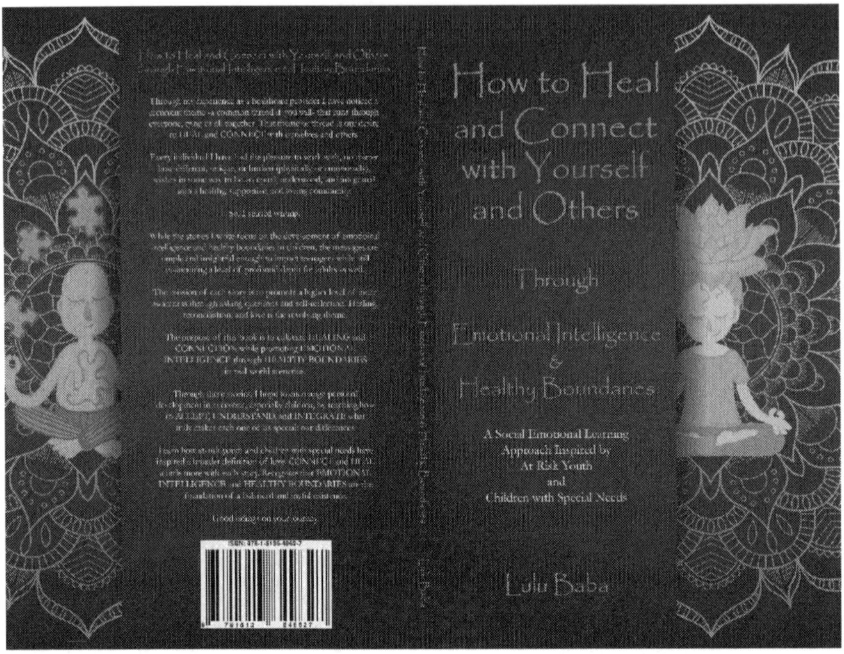
How to Heal and Connect with Yourself and Others
Through
Emotional Intelligence
&
Healthy Boundaries
A Social Emotional Learning Approach Inspired by At Risk Youth and Children with Special Needs
Lulu Baba

Celebrate Being Different
By
Lulu Baba
COLORING STORY BOOK
www.LuluBabaBooks.com
Follow young Lulu as she explores the world with her friends. Each story holds a journey of discovery and new wonders. Lulu seeks the wisdom of her grandmother, Baba, to better understand these new experiences. Baba relates to Lulu through stories that teach acceptance, understanding and integration so Lulu may learn to celebrate in all the differences of the world.
Lulu Baba COLORING STORY BOOKS embody an eco-friendly lifestyle and organic way of living. Through simple philosophy, these stories teach people young and old how to live in harmony with everyone and everything in the world today.
Come play with Lulu and Baba. Read, learn and interact through color. Make each book different and unique by painting the pages within using colors that delight you. Just remember to never be afraid to think or color outside of the lines.
Celebrate being different. – Lulu Baba
twitter
@LuluBabaBooks
Facebook.com/LuluBabaBooks
The Universe Within
Illustrated by:
Lacie Patterson
Lulu Baba

More from the Author

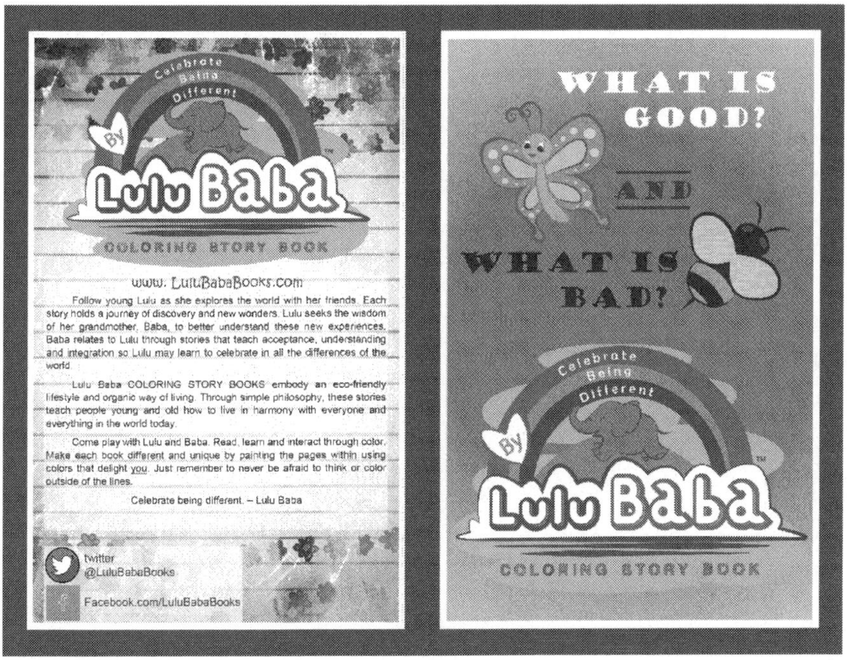

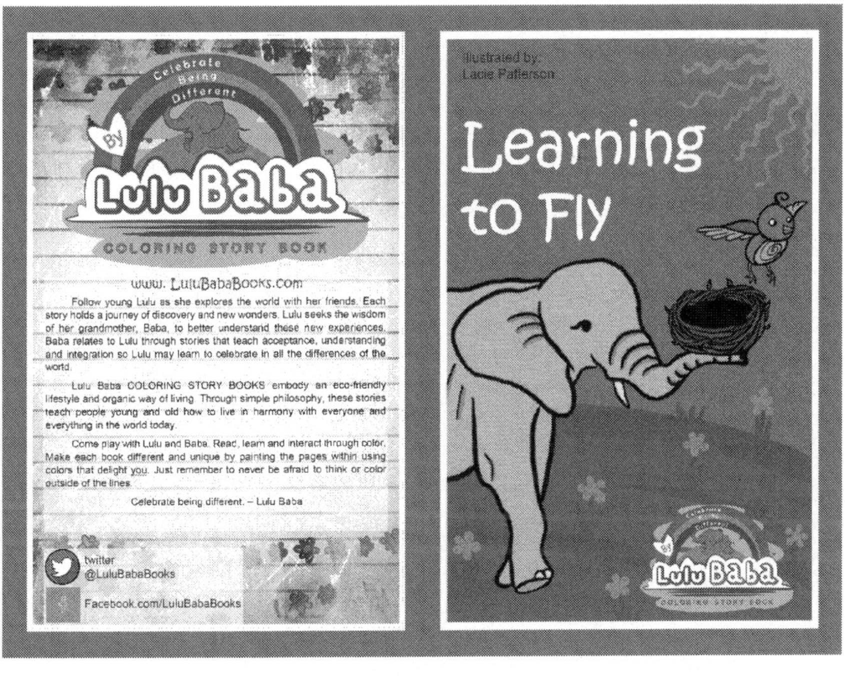

More from the Author

Made in the USA
San Bernardino, CA
13 April 2020